Y0-BSM-590

"I love to hold a vegetable
in my hand, an eggplant
or a carrot or an onion.
I love to slice it open,
hear the sound as I
cut through it, see the
beautiful patterns
inside—the seeds in
the eggplant, the layers
of the onion, the
orange flower pattern
in a carrot. I love
to beat and sift and
stir and measure
and pour . . ."

the commune cookbook

crescent dragonwagon

simon and schuster / new york

Helping to create that beautiful shuffle, friends, brothers, and sisters who put me through some changes and loved me out of others, here you are—

Michael, Ronnie, Big Diane, Little Diane, Dave, Mickey, Cheryl, the Millers, the Herbors, Junior, Alida, Dennis, Annette, Sharon Anarchos, Alternate U, Freddy, Murray, the liberated *Rat*, Florence, Genie, Ray, Danny, Peter, Joan, and Crispin—

Bob, Pete, Nancy, Lynn, Emma, Elvira, Brooklyn Duck, the Sallees, and Nubbin Ridge Sunday School— **1650830**

Bob, Mark P, Gary, Meg, Electric Al, Kim, Susan K, Suzie B, Sherry Jo, Julia, Steve Madog, Michaels Y and R, Rush, Bruce, Marc S, Beanblossom, Daryl, Leah, Warren, Lou, Trasher, Bill Bergdorf, Leftbank Books, the Outlaw, the Loop, and Pratzaels stoned out at two in the morning—

Understanding that times change, understanding the need for a balance between struggle and flow, thanking you, I wish for you and all of us love and freedom—

crescent

contents

introduction

Intro, says my neat little outline. Begin at beginning. The beginning then of the cookbook, as well as a lot of other things, was officially May 1, 1969. That was the day our lease began. I say officially because in reality, Crispin and I moved in about two weeks prior to that, Mike and Ronnie moved in about two weeks later than that, and the Dianes moved in about a month later. I'm not sure when Mickey moved in—probably around the same time Mike and Ronnie did.

It all really began at Alternate U. Four in our midst were attending a class there—in anarchism. Michael and Ronnie and Little Diane were there. Mike and Ronnie had lived together for four years, and Diane was their long-time friend from California. They wanted to live in a commune, and they were looking for people to do it with. They met Crispin, and Crispin met them, and all four of them really liked each other. A little after that Crispin and I met. We really liked each other, too. In fact, we fell in love with each other. Later, I met Mike and Ronnie. I liked them, but I still thought a commune was a dumb idea. I'd hate it. I wouldn't fit in. I wished I could talk Crispin out of it, but he was dead set on it. What could I do? I went out to see the house with him. He, Mike, Ronnie and Little Diane had all seen it at that point. We all met there, along with a guy named John, who didn't move in, and Big Diane, who did.

The house was what won me over, actually. It was, and is, so beautiful. It's a four-story brownstone in the Fort Greene section of Brooklyn, with big rooms, high, ornate ceilings, parquet floors, chandeliers. It was really trashed then—painted dark, depressing colors, incredibly dirty and dusty, plaster on the floors, no working bathrooms. It was still beautiful. The lady who let us in was blonde, pretty, pleasant and harassed looking. She was Mrs. Miller, our landlady. The Millers would fix the bathrooms, spackle the walls, and purchase the paint, which we would then apply. The rent was 350 dollars a month.

Okay, we said, and signed the lease. We argued and then drew slips of paper to figure out what bedroom each of us would have. Everybody wound up more or less satisfied.

As I remember the only people I particularly liked (besides Crispin) were Mike and Ronnie. The Dianes didn't seem too super-nice.

Little did I know.

A lot of people ask what we had in common. The answer was, initially, nothing more than our desire to live together and to make it work. We wound up, of course, sharing much more than that in certain areas.

Our backgrounds and ages are totally diverse. The oldest of us is Michael, thirty, and the youngest, me, sixteen. Michael's father was an army man. Michael finished school with a degree in psych. Ronnie's father is a substitute teacher in high schools around Brooklyn and the whole family is occasionally vegetarian. She was an anthropology major. Big Diane grew up in New Jersey near Philadelphia and her cooking reveals the Pennsylvania Dutch influence of that area. She makes fantastic pottery, taught history for a while, and is now a case worker as are Ronnie and Little Diane. To clarify the Little and Big Dianes—both are fairly tall, but Big Diane is taller and very big-boned. Little Diane is very slender and delicately put together. She also has a psych degree and in another life she once thought of becoming a behavioral psychiatrist. Right now, she cooks a lot and she and I often meet in the kitchen and rap Eastern philosophy, women's liberation and revolution. Her father runs a pharmaceutical something-or-other in New York and her mother owns a fantastic little shop in San Francisco called the Gamut. (Stop in there and say you are a friend of a friend of Diane's. Her mother will dig it.) In another life, Crispin was assistant to the state archaeologist of Texas until he got busted for grass in Mexico and spent nine months in jail there which pretty much changed his head. At any rate, he just about has a degree in anthropology, knows a lot about that and is really into it still. His parents are farmers in west Texas and are strict Southern Baptists. He and Michael make money by doing free-lance carpentry, painting and odd jobs. It is hard to write about yourself as you are (or think you are) but I can tell you what I have come out of. My parents are two writers—one writes mostly children's books and the other specializes in show business biographies. I grew up in middle-class Westchester without any religious training. My father was a communist in the thirties (he smoked dope then) but now is in Alcoholics Anonymous and considers himself a "middle-of-the-road anarchist." My mother is a children's book editor as well as a writer, and digs gardening and women's liberation. I love them both— they are really good people. And I'm a high-school dropout. Which shows, I guess, that people wind up in the same place after very different journeys to it.

The house must have exuded powerful vibrations over me, for when I left that day I immediately started feeling insecure and frightened again. I wouldn't make it. I'd fuck up and Crispin would leave me. Crispin and I talked and talked, but I was still highly dubious.

Well—in a way I guess I had a right to be. I had never lived away from home before on my own. Someone once told me that if you move your books away from home, that means you're really going, never to come back to live there again. I had never made that kind of a move. I had also never made the commitment that I had made to Crispin—or rather that we had made to each other—that we wanted to spend the rest of our lives together. I had been out with and slept with many guys before him, so I knew (and know) that this was and is different. Still, I was afraid of believing in anyone or myself *that much*. My parents were, at the time, in the process of getting divorced, after thirty-five years of marriage. Another thing was I knew I'd have to work to earn money, which I had never done. All in all, it was a lot of new things at once, and I was very frightened of it all. I made it even harder for myself than it was, thinking about it like that.

I needn't have. Moving in was so easy, once I *did* it. I just kind of rolled into place. It was as if I belonged here, as if this was my real home, to which I was returning. Now, this is not to say that it was, and is, easy. It hasn't been. There have been nearly constant struggles and conflicts and little hassles. But what I've learned, about myself, about Crispin, about people in general and *these* people in particular, far outshines the hardships. And when the lease expires, I expect that some of us will go to the country together and buy land and live together. And those of us who don't—and even if none of us do—will always and forever be a part of each other.

Change is a very peculiar thing. We are always being bombarded on all sides by stimuli that have the potential to change us. But only a very tiny percentage of them actually do. We must be at a certain stage in our development before a given thing can affect us radically or even mildly. We can see a thing every day of our lives and one day we wake up and suddenly this thing has impact on us, it takes on a new meaning in regard to us, and we change. When I moved into the house I was ready to change, ready to be affected. I didn't know it then, but every crevice of my mind was to be colored by my experience here and by things relating to that experience. I was, when I moved in, ready to be turned on to healthy food. I had been exposed to it a few times before, through old boyfriends mainly, and I either reacted against it or just ignored it. Mike, Ronnie and Little Diane were into it. They didn't push it. They just kind of quietly did it. On their nights they cooked healthy food. On my night I cooked unhealthy food. But somehow, what they were doing rubbed off on me. It made sense. I began to read about it and do it. And I still do it. And I probably will continue to do it, or some variation of it, the rest of my life. And the way it's been for me with healthy food, it's been with virtually everything.

the philosophy
of healthy food

Most people, including myself, have been administered to all their lives through by fragmented A.M.A.-believing doctors. Such doctors teach us from our earliest hours, from before we know that we are being taught, to equate health and non-illness. In other words, if you're not sick, you're well. Anyone, if they think about it, can grasp the idea that if someone is tired when he wakes up, has a backache all day, or headache, and feels constantly sluggish, that while he is not actually sick, he is not well, either. But so few of us think about it. Instead, we accept this as health. It never even enters our minds to ask for something more. Even if we did, and went to our doctor, he would probably examine us, run tests, and tell us nothing was wrong—everybody feels like that these days. And everybody does. But that doesn't make it right or inevitable. It just means that we have been very successfully brainwashed. Our nation is not nearly as healthy as we are led to believe. This is shown by our boasting about the number of hospitals that we have— forgetting that a hospital is a symbol of sickness, decay and ultimately death. Life expectancy has gone up twenty-two years since 1900—true. This is because a lot more babies died in their first year then, as opposed to less than 3 percent now. But, while infectious diseases, maternal and infant deaths have dropped, degenerative and chronic diseases have soared—arthritis, rheumatism, cancer and heart disease. Statistically; a man of forty now will live only two years longer than a man of forty in 1900. So you see, we're not healthy. We're just not sick.

But say we decide one day that we are truly sick. We have a fever or some other symptom we cannot ignore. We go to the doctor and we get diagnosed. And usually that diagnosis has something to do with *one part* of us; kidney trouble, or heart disease or strep throat. We are given to believe that one part of us can be sick and hence cured. This does not take into account the body as a whole, a complex and delicately balanced ecological system. The sickness in one part of our bodies is only a manifestation of a sickness that pervades our whole bodies. Michael, Crispin and I were watching the six o'clock news one night. They were talking to a doctor who had just operated on Senator Dirksen. The doctor said, "Yes, ah, well, we cut the cancer out of his lung and he should be all right now." "Ha!" said Michael, in a knowing and scornful way. "You don't have cancer of the lung—you have cancer of the body." A few weeks later the good Senator died.

The whole body is well or the whole body is sick. You cannot separate any part of the body from any other, just as you cannot separate any thing or person from the whole universe. This misconception—that you can—allows us to plunder our environment, to rob and exploit its ore, its water, its trees. These acts would be inconceivable if we saw ourselves as part of the universe, with trees, ore, water, our brothers and sisters. Unless this rampage is stopped and the attitudes corrected that make it possible, we will all be killed eventually. Now, if we are sick, we have been doing something wrong to the whole body; eating wrong, living in New York City, not sleeping or exercising enough. Nobody just "gets" a heart attack. A heart attack is the last link in a long, long chain that could have been prevented easily and that need never have started.

We know nothing of preventive medicine. We get "sick," we get "well." Now what do we get well with? Usually, I would say, with something unpleasant. Often, and especially often in childhood, an unpleasant-tasting medicine. We are easily conditioned—the stimulus is repeated over and over again. If it's good for you it must taste bad. We learn.

And that is why so many people are genuinely surprised when they find out that healthy food really tastes good.

Americans are a strange lot. They are not, as some people accuse, a nation of materialists, but of symbolists. This is evidenced in their attitudes toward, for instance, a painting—its "worth" often lies more in its cost, in terms of dollars and cents. A flag is, of course, nothing more than a piece of striped cloth. But burn one sometime—the effect of the destruction of a symbol on people is far, far greater than the effect of talking revolution. They (we) confuse the symbolic with the real.

This is apparent in many of our food attitudes. At a court hearing (quoted in William Longgood's *Poisons in Your Food*) on the use of red 32 dye on oranges, which

> was fed to rats at the level of 2 percent of the diet, all the rats died within a week. At a 1 percent level, death occurred within twelve days. At 0.5 percent, most rats showed marked growth retardation and anemia. Autopsy revealed moderate to marked liver damage.

The orange industry objected strenuously to banning this dye. It is still in use. It was pointed out that though oranges were picked from the tree green, by the time they were packed, shipped and unpacked, they would be ripe, though still green in color. A spokesman for the orange industry explained that people just wouldn't buy green oranges. He was probably right. But this brings several questions to mind. One is, *why* won't we eat green oranges? Well, we're symbolists. A green orange represents our inability to triumph completely over nature; we've been able to ship oranges hundreds of miles, get them to their destination ripe and fresh but—*green? Green oranges?* Forget it! But if people didn't live so far away from orange trees, they wouldn't have to be picked green and ripen in transit in the first place. They could remain on the tree until they were ripe and orange. If you didn't live in an area that oranges grew in, then you would do without oranges. Within a given natural area there will be a plant that supplies Vitamin C, if we recognize it, if not oranges, then rose hips or violet leaves or something else that we may not know is edible, just as there will surely be one sort of carbohydrate plant growing there—if not rice, then potatoes, or bananas, or wheat. This may seem primitive to us, but "primitive man had a vast number of native plans and animals at his disposal, while civilized man limits himself to a mere handful, confining his basic diet to a small number of products, an insignificant percentage of the natural varieties existing on the surface of the earth. A study of primitive populations of the Gold Coast showed that the inhabitants of one small community in that region of Africa included in their diet some 114 species of fruit, 46 species of leguminous seeds, and 47 species of greens." (Josué de Castro, *The Geography of Hunger.*) This variety is true not only of food but virtually everything. If communities, ecologically bounded (a valley, say, would be an ecological boundary), were set up, everything the community needed could be produced within that community without difficulty. Of course, there are areas where this doesn't hold true, like deserts, but once upon a time it did. Almost all desert has come about from some forgotten peoples' failure to comply with certain basic natural rules. Once fertile land has been overgrazed and mistreated and has ultimately responded by turning into arid lifeless desert, still however failing to teach man a lesson—you can't fuck nature over and over and expect her to just lie there. This is true of our food. We color it, spray it, raise it on artificially fertilized soil to make it large and nutrientless, and we pay—in ill health. Even if we choose to have our food flown in, we must learn to accept the reality of green oranges.

But really, I got off the subject. I was talking about symbolism in food. Actually, it isn't too far off the subject; the same misconceptions, the same basic attitudes cause deserts, poisoned food and symbolic acts. At any rate, another way symbolism manifests itself in food is the fact that some of our foods are associated with wealth and some with poverty. Often, the most unhealthful foods are the ones with an elitist background.

Take, for instance, white flour. But first, look at the subconscious chauvinism in the word "unrefined." Unrefined means someone uneducated, someone who doesn't know enough not to burp out loud. Unrefined also means whole wheat flour, as opposed to white flour. You see? Our language trips us up. When flour was first refined to the point of whiteness, it was of course more expensive than the regular coarse ground brown flour. Only the very rich could afford it. This goes way back; during the Roman Empire flour was ground and refined into three grades: for the slave, the middle and the ruling classes. And we all know about the Russian peasants—their black bread and cabbage soup. And closer to our own time, in the classic Laura Ingalls Wilder books—eight children's novels about life on the frontier—when Pa trades in his furs at the nearest town, he only gets a tiny package each of white flour and sugar—for "company." The family eats dark for "every day." But now, our technology has "advanced" to the point where all can afford white flour, in fact, whole wheat is often more expensive. People adopted white flour easily, initially having been trained to aspire toward it. Millers adopted white flour easily as it was less perishable and virtually immune to bug attacks. So everyone was happy, if no longer as healthy.

A tiny minority feeds the majority today. Even if industry wanted us to, we couldn't just stop using insecticides and artificial fertilizers. Let me explain. The huge farms that exist today grow thousands and thousands of one kind of plant crop in one area instead of a few each of many different kinds in small plots, as was done in former days. By doing this, the conditions for an insect population are set up, and the insect population, obligingly enough, explodes. Sprays are indeed necessary to prevent massive and total destruction of the entire crop. If smaller crops are planted, such a condition has not been set up, and while there would be a certain level of insect damage, it would not be nearly as massive as the former. Another factor that enters into this is the fertilizer used. It seems insects have a tendency to strike a more poorly nourished vegetable, one raised to lovely, big, symbolic appearance by the use of nitrates in the soil, than to attack a smaller, more nutrient-rich one, raised on manures, peat moss, and natural compost. There is a parallel in humans—when resistance is low, disease is more likely to strike. *But*—if by some miracle of modern technology we were suddenly able to grow all fruit organically, do you think we would? At this point, I think not. I believe that our desire for symbolism is strong, that we would rather have vegetables that are perfect-looking, tasteless and nutrientless than smaller, more flavorful, vitamin-rich ones that may have a worm hole. It is not a desire for beauty as such, but what we have been taught to see as beauty: unblemished, *triumph over nature*—for nature is "blemished." Women whom we have been taught to view as beautiful, taught to strive to look like, are again absolutely symmetrical, perfect, unblemished, supremely antinatural. We (women) in fact compete with each other to see who can be the most perfect. All of us, men too, wish to triumph over nature and forget our own animalness. It is to this end that we bind and deoderize ourselves, hide our freckles and tuck in our fat. It is because of this that we are embarrassed if we fart or burp in front of someone else, another animal. The views we have been taught to hold of what beauty is, in a person, vegetable or house, besides being antinatural, are uniform. Actually, antinaturalness and uniformity are synonymous, for nature is diversity. We strive to make our environment uniform: we pave the land, eradicate its natural variations. Why? We have been carefully taught, carefully conditioned, to hold these views and do these things and love them. Uniform people, as uniform land, are easier to exploit. You can do it all the same way.

The elitist thinking that pervades our eating attitudes also pervades our cooking attitudes. We are taught, subtly and not so subtly, to see cooking as inferior work, fit only (generally) for inferior persons, "unrefined" persons, women and nonwhite women especially. In general, if a man is forced by circumstances to "cook" for himself, he will survive on Campbell's soup and TV dinners rather than really cook.

Thus, men and women are both oppressed, the women more openly but the men too. Oppressed because regardless of whether or not either likes to cook, both are imprisoned in certain roles from which there is no escaping. Oppressed because in a slave/master relationship, the master is a slave too. He *must* behave the part of a master. Besides the obvious implications of the above (see Bibliography, page 181), there are several other bad results of such a setup, just as serious. (I must interject a note here. I have talked to women who feel that women's liberation is the most important political issue today; blacks who feel that black liberation is the most important issue, and people who feel that chemicals in food, or Vietnam or air pollution is the most important issue. The point is, they're all important, incredibly so. *All* are caused by the same thing, and we cannot be free of one of these issues until *all* of us are free of *all* of them, and the only way we can *all* be free of all of them is a complete change, a change so strong it eradicates the causes and the attitudes that caused the causes. People must fight in all areas, on every front. It is perhaps best for individuals to fight where they personally feel the oppression most strongly because there they can do a better job of fighting. But no person should dare to assume that his fight is the biggest one, that it supersedes all other fights, and that everybody should come and fight his way. The only issue that encompasses all these issues is ecology—the relationship of everything to everything else, for Vietnam, the oppression of women and Blacks, chemicals in food are all symptoms of a fucked-up ecology, or rather the symptoms of a system so fucked up as to be unaware of ecology, unaware of the relationships in this wide cosmos, only aware of its individual self and that self's needs. That change, then, the revolution, equals a sane ecology. Ecology is primarily a social issue.) At any rate, women know that cooking is work, that it is something that must be done every day, and the dishes washed afterwards. It is a chore, something to be done quickly to get it over with (though some women are so thoroughly brainwashed-bored that they will spend all day every day cooking for their families, something I would never do), something to hate doing. The result—tense women and unhealthy food—because unhealthy food is so often "instant." Healthy foods can be cooked as elaborately or simply, in as long or short length of time, as unhealthy foods, but women who are forced to cook will not be interested enough in cooking to investigate healthy versus unhealthy food; often they will just buy instant, prepared, ready-to-use pre-packaged shit, thinking they are buying freedom. Men also know that cooking is a drag and women's work, also to be done quickly, if at all, and winding up unhealthily. And besides the end result of such a system, in health, that is, men and women both lose out on something deeply important, and that is the great sensual pleasure in cooking.

Man, I love to cook. I love to hold a vegetable in my hand, an eggplant or a carrot or an onion. I love to slice it open, hear the sound as I cut through it, note the difference between the outside and inside of it, see the beautiful patterns inside, the seeds in the eggplant, the layers of the onion, the orange star-flower pattern in a carrot. I love to beat and sift and stir and measure and pour. I love putting together all these good in-gredients and watching them turn into something new. I love to pull meat from the bone and sample a bit, raw, as I go along, or to arrange a platter, contrasting white cottage cheese and green flecks of chives and carrot and celery and sliced cucum-ber winding up with something a delight to look at, a delight to eat. Cooking is, or can be, a fantastically creative, expressive art, and I argue fervently with someone who tells me otherwise. If you don't like to cook, ask yourself why. Is it a response to certain roles society has tried to force you into? Remember, *all* children love to "cook," mixing mud and grass and leaves, pat-ting it into little cakes and sprinkling them with sand and marigold petals. I wish everyone could find the same deep joy in cooking now that they did twenty or thirty or forty years ago when they were that much more innocent. In fact, the same deep joy in everything. I feel sorry for people who tell me how much more creative an act writing a poem or painting a picture is. They have never really cooked. As is obvious, I write too, and not only cookbooks, and yes, it satisfies me to write but so does cooking. Why confine your creative acts to one realm? If you truly strive to free yourself, you will find everything you do to be a freeing act.

mechanics

A while ago this guy came to visit us from another commune. I must confess I took an almost immediate dislike to him. He struck me as an organizer and an interrupter, both types of people I have no affinity for. He was interested, at any rate, in setting up communication between various communes. We were talking about various things, about how our respective groups worked, shopping and cleaning up and so forth. We asked how his group did their cooking and he replied, rather nonchalantly, "Well, we used to just cook whenever somebody felt like it, but a few days ago somebody got uptight and decided we had to eat every day."

Obviously, you have to eat every day, but we manage not to get uptight about it at all. In fact, we really dig it. Meals are where we get together most often. We talk and eat and catch up on what's happening with each other and the world. Somebody different cooks every night and somebody else washes the dishes. This is all figured out at the Sunday night meeting, which is sometimes on Monday or Tuesday, but usually on Sunday. People decide what night they can cook and what they're going to make. They make up a list of what ingredients they need and submit it to the shoppers for that week. The shoppers compile a list of all the other lists and rumble around the kitchen a little to see what staples we're out of or low on, and what spices. Then, the following day, the shoppers shop, in Mike and Ronnie's microbus, or Big Diane's jeep, loading the bags and bags of stuff in and driving from place to place (see Shopping, page 173) until finally they head home, often getting caught in the five o'clock rush hour traffic, but finally making it to Brooklyn, banging on the door, yelling for someone to open it and come carry the stuff in. Then, the parade begins: from car to kitchen go four or five of us and a few neighborhood kids. All in the kitchen, we start unpacking the stuff, transferring the spices (after figuring out what each one is) from the tiny folded-over brown paper bags to the appropriate jar, pouring the flour from huge sacks into the plastic garbage cans used to store it in, putting the eggs into their little nests in the refrigerator, putting water on to boil for tea, and all the while the shoppers regaling us with stories of what happened. Almost always something does happen—either the guy gives us a whole load of free cheese or some cans that cottage cheese comes in, or we get stopped and harassed by the police for some nonsensical thing (we never get a ticket; they just hassle us a little and let us go with a warning never again to do whatever it is they've decided we've done). Or something. And meanwhile everybody is putting stuff away, and the kids too, opening little bags and saying in a tone of disgust, "What's *that?*" "Peppermint tea." "Yeeechh!" "What's *that?*" "Wheat germ." "Yeeechh," and then, "That's to keep you from getting sick from whole wheat flour?" This is just a dumb joke on Junior's part. He and I have a running battle over which is better: whole wheat flour or white flour. Days when we don't go shopping, Junior and/or James and Dennis come over around five o'clock to see what's doing. Often I am baking bread at that time, and they have learned how. At any rate, that's how we work the cooking. That, along with somebody washing the dishes each night, are really the only structured jobs we have. Cleaning just gets done. If something's dirty enough to be impractical, or dirty enough to bother you—you clean it. That works out pretty well too.

Also at the Sunday night meeting the bills are gone over. Telephone bills are done by reading the names of the places any long-distance calls have been to: "Omaha, Nebraska?" "That's me." People pay for their individual long-distance phone calls. Then the cost of all the long distance phone calls are added together and subtracted from the total and that figure divided eight ways—unless someone has made an especially large number of local calls, in which case the bill is rearranged accordingly. I go into this in such detail because we heard of a new commune that was going to have eight separate phone numbers because they hadn't figured out a way to do it otherwise! Other bills are just generally divided eight ways.

Sunday nights group problems are also brought up. Usually these are not so much problems as things that need to be decided on, like should we start buying organic food; or I think it would be nice if we had a party such and such a time, could we; or nobody uses that big desk in the living room—I really need one, could I take it up to my room? This last was something I brought up. I was, finally, awarded the desk, a beautiful rolltop one I fell in love with the first day I saw the house. I was not allowed to have it initially because it was thought that people would use it if it was left in the hall. They didn't. I brought the desk question up again. Everybody said it was just that the hall was an inconvenient place and it should be moved to the living room. So it was, but nobody used it. So I asked, yet again, if I could have it in my room. Mind you, it was something like five months after I had brought it up the first time. People agreed, nobody was using it, though it *did* look nice. So it was given to me. There's a moral here: something about patience.

Problems that concern individuals are usually hassled out when they occur. That's very important in regard to living with someone, anyone, one person or a lot of people. If someone does something that annoys you, talk to them about it *immediately*. Why did you do that? What did you mean by that? And, once you've started, finish. Otherwise, it will lie there, inside both of you, ready to come shooting out at the next problem. An indication of how sane a given two people that know each other are is to listen to them fight. Do they fight about one thing? Or do they go back to his high school grades and her old boyfriends and his trip to Paris and so on and so forth. Usually our fights are about what they are. You've heard people fight about one thing when it's quite obvious they mean another. I don't think we do that, at least not often. If one of us starts to, the others(s) will say, "Hey, what are you doing?" I cannot overemphasize how important I think it is to fight honestly. A good fight can be one of the most constructive of all things, and I really believe in them.

So, that's the way the house works, and it really works well. Part of it has been luck—in finding the house itself, having such good landlords, and just our happening to all be at a stage where we could grow more productively together than separately. But much of it has been, as I said earlier, incredibly hard work. Being honest when you have been brought up in a manner that constantly implies that you should gloss over the truth or hide it completely or play games is not easy. I have thought many times this past year about leaving the house, and I guess, at one time or another, everybody has. But we've stuck it out and the times when it's been difficult are fewer than the times when it's been easy and fun and everybody is smiling and making jokes and feeling good and getting high and nobody being left out.

ingredients

Part two of Mechanics (which this is, in case you hadn't noticed) is going to be basic definitions and practical bits of knowledge. I'm going to talk about what I think healthy food is and explain some ingredients, which, unless you are into healthy food, you won't know about, and to tell you about what we consider good utensils.

Healthy food, simply stated, is food that makes you function more efficiently. Efficiently means fewer colds, clearer skin, not breathing hard after running up a flight of stairs. For reasons explained earlier, people figure that if a certain diet can do all this, it must taste bad. Not true! Healthy food (as opposed to Health Food, which in my mind has an entirely different connotation) is delicious, no ifs, except of course if you cook it wrong, which is no harder than cooking unhealthy food right. It *is* true that if all you have been eating is Wonder Bread and marshmallows, it will initially taste funny. But you'll get used to it, as I did, in about a month, and then, you'll never be able to go back. What I consider healthy food, in the first place, is not that weird or radically different from what most people eat. I am not a vegetarian, nor am I macrobiotic. I don't eat solely brown rice or solely seaweed, or solely anything. I eat a varied and good-tasting diet. It's basically high in protein, consisting of lots of eggs, plus good amounts of meat, organ meats, too, poultry, seafood and soybeans. I eat lots of vegetables, a good percentage of them raw, and especially favor leafy green ones. I eat a salad nearly every day. I also eat a lot of fruit, preferring citrus and fruits with yellow insides like apricots and peaches to fruits with a white pulp, like apples and pears. The yellow-fleshed ones have more food value. I also consume a lot of dairy products. The house buys about 12 pounds of cheese a week, which is usually gone by Friday, but I probably eat less of it than anyone. I prefer the so-called "low fat" cheeses, like cottage cheese, for again they have more protein. However I like the others too—cheddar, muenster, Swiss. . . . The one food group I try to eat less of is the carbohydrates. Those that I do eat are unrefined—brown, unhusked rice, potatoes with their skins, whole wheat grains. Once a sugar freak, I have now replaced refined sweeteners with honey, molasses or raw sugar. I prefer the cold-pressed variety of oils to the usual kind, as they have not been extracted from their source by harsh chemicals, such as hexane used in average commercial oils. While I still like butter and eat some, I eat less than I once did.

Now, the big difference between that and an ordinary diet, as you can see, is that it's high in protein and contains no refined or processed foods. They are bad news (see Bibliography). Another difference is I prefer *all* of what I eat to be grown organically, although this is not always possible. In the case of fruits and vegetables and grains, organic means grown free of insecticides, on naturally fertilized soil, with manure, compost, and peat moss being used instead of nitrates. It means that after the vegetables and fruits are harvested they are not sprayed with a mold retarder or dyed or waved with a coal tar compound (or anything for that matter). Compare two cucumbers, one organic and one nonorganic. You can really tell that the nonorganic one has been waxed; it's shiny and you can scrape the wax off with your fingernail. Anyhow, organic animals and animal products mean that the stock has been fed on grains grown as described above. They have not been given antibiotics, tranquilizers, and/or sex hormones to help them gain quick, cheap, fast weight.

Not only do most organic foods taste infinitely better (there are some exceptions: we got some organic romaine lettuce that was really fucked over; it doesn't ship well), but they are much healthier for you. Besides containing fewer poisons, they contain more vitamins and nutrients than those raised on devitalized soil or grain. And wild plants contain more than the garden varieties of the same plant.

Besides taste and appearance, often smaller and less "perfect" than supermarket fruit, there is no way you can really tell if something is organic or not unless you grow it yourself, which is actually a pretty good idea and a logical one. The person eating healthy food will eventually come to the conclusion that he wants to live in a healthy environment and get lots of exercise every day. But, until you reach that conclusion, and if, indeed, you never do, the best thing to do is to start an organic food co-op. The basic reason to do this is because organic food is damned expensive and if you get fifty or sixty people together they can buy it wholesale cheaper than at your ordinary exploitative, run-of-the-mill Health Food Store.

The co-op we're involved in, of which Little Diane and Ronnie did the original coordination, is centered at Alternate U. It works on an order basis: you place your order and it comes the following week, on Mondays, when you must be over at Alternate U. to pick it up. It is completely nonprofit; there is initially only a two dollar fee required to pay for supplies like paper bags and scales. That is paid once and never again. Needless to say such an operation requires much bookkeeping and time, too—calling in orders, taking orders, distributing food. The only way this can be done, without profit, is for each of the sixty people involved to coordinate one week each and teach it to someone new the next week. It has really worked out well for us. In fact, a group at Columbia is starting one on the same principle. So, unless you're *quite* rich, consider starting or participating in such a thing. If you're in a large city, look in the telephone book under Health Foods for a supplier, or write directly to farms listed in *Organic Shopping and Living:* one dollar, Emmaus, Pennsylvania. This is better because it eliminates a middleman and is cheaper and less alienated.

And now I shall introduce you to some ingredients with which you may not be familiar.

The first is *nutritional yeast*. This amazing substance, also according to its form called brewer's, torula, or food yeast, is a by-product of the brewing process. At least it was before it was found to be a potent source of the B Vitamins and a high-protein food. Much of it is now grown specifically as a food substance, in molasses to make it more palatable. It really tastes bad by itself but can be stirred into many things without detrimental effect. Brewer's tastes the worst and has the least nutritional value. Torula, food, or nutritional are better on both counts. Our favorite brand is Plus Products Formula 250. It tastes best and has in it, according to the label, per heaping tablespoonful:

MINERALS

Calcium	240 mgs.	Magnesium	150 mgs.
Phosphorus	240 mgs.	Zinc	2 mgs.
Iron	2.8 mgs.	Sodium	2.4 mgs.
Copper	.28 mgs.	Potassium	320 mgs.
Iodine	.67 mgs.	Manganese	.56 mgs.

VITAMIN B COMPLEX FACTORS

Vitamin B-1	4 mgs.	Pantothenic Acid	16 mgs.
Vitamin B-2	4 mgs.	Para-aminobenzoic	
Vitamin B-6	4 mgs.	Acid	16 mgs.
Niacin	40 mgs.	Choline	44 mgs.
Vitamin B-12	8 mcgs.	Inositol	64 mgs.
		Biotin	25 mcgs.

Any nutritionist will tell you that getting all this in 1 tablespoonful is no mean thing. There are in addition some 5–10 grams of protein in a tablespoon of brewer's yeast, so one-fourth cup supplies one-third the minimum daily requirement for women. So—use it! I mean, what can I say? Incidentally, it is not a baking yeast and will not cause anything to rise (except your Vitamin B intake)!

GRANULAR KELP is a powdered seaweed and it is delicious sprinkled on salads, on some soups and with eggs. Use it where recipes call for it. It is available at any health food store, and is a rich natural source of iodine and other trace minerals. Also, if you're out of salt, a bit less than double the measure of kelp can be substituted.

SEA SALT is preferable to any other kind because it, too, has many trace minerals and does *not* have certain anticaking agents added, whose effect on the human body is unknown.

NON-INSTANT POWDERED MILK is not too good for drinking (tastewise), and nutrientwise it should not be substituted for fresh except when you're out and it's Sunday night and the little *bodega* on the corner is closed. It can be used a lot in cooking. It is much higher in protein than flour (any kind except soy flour) and can be substituted for some of it in many recipes. It can also be used to bind meat loaf and the like. It is better for cooking with than the instant which has a much coarser texture and gets gummy when heated.

WHEAT GERM is a high-protein food, also high in the B-Vitamins, which is good to cook with too, substituting it for part flour. Get the raw, untoasted type, as some nutrients are destroyed by heating. I was reading about an experiment where they gave squirrels unlimited amounts of whole wheat grain. After a while the squirrels began to crack the grain open, eat the germ, and throw away the rest, the little devils.

COLD-PRESSED OILS are preferable to the Wesson variety as they are 1) extracted from the plant without being heated, or heated at very low heat, thus preserving nutrients, and because 2) they do not have any preservatives added except, in some cases, Vitamin E. They should be refrigerated after being opened. These oils contain substances: lecithin and inositol, unsaturated fatty acids, that is, that help break down that nightmare of the American diet, cholesterol.

And now that I have more or less accounted for myself, I present the recipes.

soups

Soups are one of the cheapest, best tasting, and easiest things to make. Of course, there *are* soups that are expensive, not particularly good and difficult to make, but we do not concern ourselves with such obviously elite substances.

It is essential to save any water that you cook vegetables, meat, chicken or fish in. They can be poured into one or several mason jars and will keep quite a while in the refrigerator. Also save any part of a vegetable that you might usually throw out, like carrot tops and peelings, lettuce cores and outer leaves, onion ends, pea pods, etcetera. *Don't throw anything out without thinking of this.* All these can sit in a large plastic garbage bag or a pitcher in the refrigerator. However, do this only with organic vegetables. There are good reasons for this. In the first place, as most people know, most of the vitamins and minerals lie directly under the skins in most fruits and vegetables—skins that we probably normally throw out. However, in nonorganic vegetables most of the pesticides and sprays *also* collect directly under the skin, with dyes and waxes, of course, right on the skin. Now does it make sense? Too, organic stuff is so much more costly than the other—not a scrap of it should be wasted.

END-OF-THE-WEEK SOUP

At any rate, at the end of the week, or if you are poor and temporarily penniless, consolidate all the saved cooking waters and vegetables in a large pot. It should look kind of garbagey and it should be thick with scraps (you will really be amazed to see how many things you once, oh so carefully, threw out). Salt well, to draw out the flavor of the vegetables. Add a bay leaf, some basil, some oregano, some rosemary, a clove of garlic, some kelp. Simmer for about fifteen minutes, covered. This is long enough! Longer cooking will serve no purpose save to destroy vitamins. It will probably be quite bland tasting, but never fear. Store it in the refrigerator for a few hours, or better yet, overnight. Lo and behold: it will be more spicy and good. Why? The flavor of the herbs will have passed into the cooking water. Strain it now (it's absurd to strain a huge quantity of boiling hot liquid, as I found out one sad day). At this point it is ready to be used as stock in any recipe calling for same, or to continue on its way as End-of-the-Week Soup.

If you chose the latter path, add to it a few of whatever grains you have lying around (and you should always have some), such as brown rice or lentils. Simmer this till these are almost done. Now, add some neatly chopped carrots, onions, celery. How different it looked yesterday! If you didn't add grains, add a potato, with skin, diced or sliced. If you vote against either grain or potato, add some noodles, but bear in mind that the other starches are better for you. A can or two of tomatoes or tomato sauce or tomato paste will completely change the flavor of this soup, sometimes for the better, sometimes not. Beets are more risky, but a core, or a few fresh, washed beets will also change the flavor.

In about ten minutes you have—End-of-the-Week Soup! It is nearly always good and is excellent with one of the garnishes mentioned at the end of this chapter (*see* page 35). Since it should (or at least can—must, if you are poor) be made fairly often, once a week or so, try all these variations, though no-body will really be fooled.

A little psychology will help—give your soup a name. Add canned tomatoes and some Savoy cabbage, some string beans and some zucchini and some cooked kidney beans. Serve it with garlic bread and top it with grated cheese and parsley and call it—you guessed it—Minestrone. Or add lots of lentils, some curry powder, some onions, some celery, some carrots, a little tomato paste and call it Mulligatawny. Or add cabbage, onions, carrots and beets (go heavy on the first and last). Season generously with dill and garnish with a blob of sour cream in each person's bowl. Serve with black bread. What is it, folks? Borscht! As you can see, these are the illegitimate children of their namesakes, and while they will infuriate snobs, they will please most peasants. A warning—whichever variation you choose, even if you are trying to use up all those things which have been lurking on your shelf for an eternity—*don't* throw in canned soup. No matter how big your honorable brew may be proportionately, the canned soup will permeate it quite totally. Friends, experience has been my teacher. And beware of bouillon cubes, too. All commercial varieties I have seen contain monosodium glutamate (of course, nearly all commercial anythings do). However, at a health food store you can purchase some healthful vegetable, chicken or beef powder, MSG-less. But read the label; some brands there have it too. We use Sherman Arcadia. It's expensive, but a two-dollar jar lasts a long time. This powder can be used to spruce up certain sauces and soups, with discretion. And what is MSG? Just a chemical shown to cause brain damage in mice. At the time of the cyclamate commotion, there was a wee bit of noise about it, but it was soon dropped. At any rate, avoid it.

Dried lentil and split pea soups are something Big Diane first turned me, in fact everybody here, on to. They are also cheap, and do not require much work to be tasty.

BIG DIANE'S SPLIT PEA SOUP
(thick as London fog)

Cover
> 1 pound split peas
> 4 or 5 ham hocks (or other ham bones and scraps)

With
> Just enough vegetable water or plain water to cover
> Salt, pepper
> Thyme
> Basil

Simmer this for forty-five minutes to an hour, mushing occasionally with a wooden spoon if you like, and adding more liquid should it become necessary.

Now add
> 3 carrots, chopped (with skins)
> 3 stalks celery, chopped
> 1 onion, chopped

Simmer about fifteen to twenty minutes more. To shorten cooking time the peas may be soaked overnight, in which case the herbs should be added to the soaking water.

Vinegar, which would extract the calcium from the hocks, unfortunately toughens the split peas as well. Forget it or use previously prepared stock.

This makes a thick soup. Of course, it can be thinned down by adding more water. A variation of this is to use a pound of lentils instead of split peas and about a tablespoonful of molasses, following the same recipe. Both the pea and lentil soups are quite substantial and require nothing more than perhaps a salad with cheese and hard-boiled eggs cut into it, and some whole wheat toast, to be a full meal, a very full meal, I might add. End-of-the-Week Soup is what you make it—main dish, first course, or snack.

CHICKEN BROTH

And now is the time to learn how to make a good, flavorful chicken broth. You will find you use it a lot, to stew the meat off the bones, or just because you need the broth. If you're making it specifically to use the meat in something else, bring the water to a boil first, turn down the heat, then put in the chicken. This helps seal the flavor *in*. Otherwise,

Cover with water

A chicken or ½ pound chicken feet, which supply good color and flavor and are dirt cheap

Add to the water

Salt, pepper, celery seed, sage, a bay leaf, basil, rosemary, whatever . . .

A few each: carrots, celery, garlic clove(s)

2 onions, quartered, with a few cloves stuck in one of the quarters

Simmer gently over low heat (high heat will toughen it) at least till the broth is fragrant, rich and chickeny, and the bird itself is tender. This will be somewhere between one and three hours depending upon the age of the chicken. You may wish to stew it even longer, till the meat falls off the bones, perhaps. It depends what you're using it for. In the first hour of cooking, a nasty-looking scum will keep appearing, most persistently. Just skim it off and keep skimming until it doesn't appear any more. You may, if all you need is broth, use only feet.

ASOPAO DE POLLO

This is kind of a Spanish chicken soup-stew, given to me by Julia Vasquez, who lives down the street, along with Alida and Dennis and Annette.

Just barely cover with water

A chicken, cut in pieces

Add

> Salt, pepper
> ½ bunch celery
> 2 tomatoes, peeled and chopped
> ½ bag carrots
> 4 cloves garlic
> About 10 *ajíes y recao* (these are small, roundish, pale green things, not hot, available all over New York in Spanish groceries. As far as I know they have no English name)
> 1 or 2 red hot peppers, *picantes* in Spanish—add these if you want your soup hot

Cook over low heat until tender, about an hour. Meanwhile, cook separately

> 1 cup rice

Mrs. Vasquez uses white but she sees no reason why brown should not be used, so we do. When the chicken is tender, you may strain the broth, or you can leave it as is. The chicken is usually left on the bones, but it may be picked off if you like. Mix the rice with the broth and chicken.

Now add

> 1 can tomato sauce
> 2 teaspoons lard or other fat, or butter

Simmer covered until fairly thick, like a thick soup, and the chicken and rice are quite soft. Serve with green bananas and baked sweet potatoes. This is a Puerto Rican winter dinner.

FRUIT SOUP
(Sot soppa)

This sounds weird, but it's really delicious. It is hard to give quantities on this, for it too is a sort of end-of-the-week soup.

Bring to a boil

> A large quantity of juice

Berry juices are best, cranberry, or raspberry or black cherry (try the Hain organic concentrates, if you're rich or work in a health food store where you can liberate such luxuries), but others will do.

Now add to it any of the following fruits

> Dried apricots (a lot)
> Raisins, gold and dark
> Pitted prunes (a fair amount)   **1650830**
> Chopped cooking apples
> Strawberries, raspberries, rhubarb (all or none)
> Orange sections

Season with

> 1 cinnamon stick, cut in two
> Peel of ½ each organic lemon and orange, grated
> 1 slice ginger root, or a piece of crystallized ginger

Simmer gently for half an hour or less, till the dried fruits plump up but the apples are not mushy. Taste it. If it seems too thick, thin it with water or more juice.

If your particular blend of taste buds call for sweetening, do so with

> Honey, raw sugar, or jam (preferably in that order)

This soup may be served warm or cold, winter or summer. If you serve it cold, you may add a few sliced bananas before serving. Don't add them too soon before serving or they will become mushy. This soup tends to be a peculiar cerise-brown color, but don't be alarmed. It is whatever you make it, but whatever you make it, it is extremely laxative.

garnishes

Garnish is a pretty, delicate word and is what it sounds like, something to go on top of something to make it look pretty and/or tastier and/or healthier. Most of them you know, at least the starting ones, but I put them here in case you are very flustered and have temporarily forgotten, as I sometimes do.

> Paper-thin slices of lemon, carrot, radish, cucumber, zucchini

Slices or cubes of tofu (bean curd)

Finely chopped fresh parsley, watercress, dill, or chives

Grated Parmesan cheese

Finely chopped hard-boiled eggs

Bacon, cooked crisply and then crumbled

Chopped nuts and seeds

Blobs of sour cream or yogurt

Any kind of sprout

Grated coconut

Sliced crisp apple

Tiny fingers of fresh pineapple

Toasted wheat germ

Flecks of certain spices on cream soups—nutmeg, paprika, curry. Of course not all of these are good for all soups. But you know that surely, and you know which fit where.

Now we come to some more interesting garnishes, namely dumplings. These require more preparation than the above, but they can transform a plain old broth into something better (a plain old broth with dumplings).

LIGHT WHOLE WHEAT DUMPLINGS

Scald and cool to lukewarm
　　1 cup milk
In it, dissolve
　　1 tablespoon dried yeast
Let stand a few moments and beat in
　　2 eggs
　　1 teaspoon each salt and honey and brewer's yeast
　　1 tablespoon each milk powder and wheat germ
　　1 to 2 cups whole wheat flour—enough to make a very soft dough

Let this rise until doubled or nearly doubled in bulk. Stir down. Now, scoop out blobs of dough, about a quarter cup per blob, and drop into a dish of whole wheat flour. Roll around therein and form into a dumpling (the flour keeps it from sticking to you and its brothers and sisters). Place on a platter, covered, in a warm place and let rise again. Have a large pot of soup stock boiling. Turn the heat down to a good simmer and gently drop the dumplings in one by one. Cover and simmer for about fifteen minutes.

VARIATION: cook in hot milk or water and use to accompany pot roast or the like. Or serve with stewed fruit for a rich dessert.

appetizers

Appetizers are really pleasant. They can be juice or fish or meat or cheese or fruit or vegetable-based. But, whatever they are, they can save you when people are zooming into the kitchen to snack on filling things when dinner is half an hour away and you want them to wait but they are being difficult. An appetizer platter can be made with no difficulty out of stuff you have around. Again, it's just a matter of disguising it to look new and different and pretty. First, you might cut some cheese into cubes—a softish one like muenster is better than a sharp one for this—and dip one side of it in caraway seeds. Arrange the cubes on the platter. Now slice several big mushrooms, across stem and all, so that they look nice. Sprinkle them all over with lemon juice, black pepper and a little salt. Arrange them, too. Now slice hard-boiled eggs. A dab of mayonnaise on these, a sprig of parsley, a dash of paprika. Place them neatly.

Now make a dip by combining 3 parts cottage cheese to a little less than one part mayonnaise. Add several finely chopped scallions, including green tops, and about half a carrot, grated, if you like. Season with salt, dry mustard, caraway, and kelp. Put a scoop of the dip on the platter and surround with green pepper wedges, cucumber slices and carrot sticks, for dipping. Who could ask for anything more? These are all ingredients that you probably have. If you want to plan ahead, you could add artichoke hearts, either bottled and marinated or frozen or canned plain. If you get the frozen, cook them first and then chill them, still plain or, if you like, in French dressing or plain oil and parsley or mint.

You could add celery stuffed with a mixture of cream and blue cheese, mixed together and sprinkled with marjoram. (Or stuff it with peanut butter, unhydrogenated, thinned with a little honey, and studded with raisins.) You can get whole pimientoes, spread them out and lay anchovies across them. You can make little shish kebabs on toothpicks with a slice of banana, a broiled shrimp, (previously marinated, if you like, in pineapple-grapefruit juice, seasoned with dill and oregano, or cinnamon) and an orange section.

You can compose a cheese spread of about 1 part cream cheese beaten together with 2 parts grated sharp cheddar and seasoned with caraway seeds, Worcestershire sauce, and sherry. Other grated cheeses may be added—any you have. Form the cheese spread into a ball and surround with carrot sticks, coming out like spokes (or rays). You can make a little pile of plain old tuna fish, or some shrimp mixed with mayonnaise, lemon juice, finely chopped celery, carrot, and onion. Do not forget radishes, sliced or quartered, and a little dab of a tart jam or marmalade is wonderful mixed with plain cottage cheese. Cucumbers can be sliced very thin, laid out in layers on top of each other, and sprinkled with lemon juice and basil.

Well, I hope I have given you some ideas. If you don't like them, I suppose you can always use grapefruit.

ANGELED EGGS
(as opposed to Deviled Eggs)

This next is my pet recipe.
It's hard to give exact proportions for these.

> Split some hard-boiled eggs lengthwise. Mash the yolks with plenty of mayonnaise, dry mustard, a dash of Tabasco, a little pickle relish and/or catsup,

salt, pepper, cinnamon (just a fleck or two), a small
amount of brown sugar, some nutritional yeast, and
a little minced onion. Mound this back into the
whites and sprinkle with paprika. Anything you like
may be added to this—leftover minced chicken, or
tuna or chopped olives or celery or carrots.

GUACAMOLE

This is somewhere between a dip and a salad. There are
many opinions within the house as to how it should be made—
should it be spicy or not. Well, you must decide.
Pit
    An avocado, a ripe, soft, squishy one
Scoop out the green flesh of it, mash well and add
    1 tomato, chopped
    1 small onion, chopped
    Salt and pepper
    Juice of ¼ lemon or lime or some vinegar
Now these next are optional. Some of us like some, some
others.
    Nutmeg or chili powder
    1 clove garlic, finely minced
Serve as a salad or dip, with good vegetable dippers or
crackers for dipping. If you are not serving it right away, keep
the pit buried in the prepared guacamole; it will help keep it
from browning.

These next dips are Middle Eastern and we first had them
in a great, cheap restaurant on Atlantic Avenue near here.

BABA GANOUJ

(Serve it with Damascus whole wheat bread which people tear
off in big chunks and dip in. It is not as filling as it sounds.)
Bake an eggplant at 350° F. for about an hour, first pricking
its skin well all over with a fork, to prevent exploding. Cool.

Skin and mash the flesh, including the seeds, with

> 4 tablespoons sesame tahini (this is a ground sesame seed paste, similar to peanut butter)
>
> ½ cup water
>
> 2-4 cloves garlic, pressed
>
> Juice of a lemon, or more than that
>
> Salt and pepper to taste

Blend till smooth and thick/thin. Put in dollops on a small plate, spread with spoon to form a circle and sprinkle with

> 1 or 2 tablespoons olive oil
>
> 1 or 2 tablespoons pine nuts browned in butter
>
> Parsley and paprika

Let stand awhile before serving to let the flavors permeate and marry with each other. The longer the dip is allowed to sit the less garlic is needed.

VARIATION: hommos is made in more or less the same fashion, with cooked chick peas—about three or four cups—substituted for the eggplant. The olive oil treatment is omitted.

WHOLE WHEAT MIDDLE EASTERN BREAD

This is quite a big deal to make, and unless you really dig cooking or Middle Eastern food I wouldn't advise it. You can, however, double this recipe, which is a pretty large one anyhow, and freeze most of it to use as you will.

Dissolve

> 4 tablespoons yeast

In

> 4 cups lukewarm water, or potato water, or milk, scalded and cooled to lukewarm

In a large bowl, mix together

> 9 cups whole wheat flour
>
> 1 tablespoon salt

Add this to the yeast-water mixture and also add

> 2 tablespoons rose water or orange flower water
>
> 1 tablespoon honey

Mix very well, turn into clean, oiled bowl, cover and let rise about three hours in a warm place. Turn out and divide into pieces the size of large oranges. Smooth into balls and let rise, covered, draft-free, another hour. Now roll out dough into a circle about half an inch or so in thickness. Let rise yet again —this is the third rising now. Preheat the oven to 450° F. When it has reached that heat—allow about 15 minutes—place as many loaves as you can on a cookie sheet which need not be greased but can be sprinkled lightly with cornmeal. This will probably be about two loaves. Now bake, but only about seven minutes! And watch them closely so they do not burn. Remove from the oven, put another two in, and brown the first two quickly under the broiler, about two minutes on each side, but keep an eye on them. When you have completed this process with all the "loaves" you are done and have a realio trulio healthio batch of Middle Eastern bread on your hands. (You can buy it but *not* the whole wheat form.)

Another school of the appetizer realm of thought is the *canapé*. These are little open sandwiches—a piece of toast or cracker spread with something. There are quite a few disadvantages in making them, the first being that they must be made almost immediately before serving or they will grow depressingly soggy. Another thing about them is that no matter what you do to them they always look like the front of a cracker box. My advice is that if you wish to persist in the canapé folly, have a few dishes with different kinds of crackers and let people make them themselves. This way you don't have to worry about sixty little garnishes, either.

LIVER SPREAD
(call it pâté, if you like)

To make a liver spread, grind cooked leftover liver with onions, carrots, mushrooms, garlic, and water. Crumble cooked bacon into the mixture. Use milk powder and/or wheat germ to bind it to a spreadable consistency. For a fancier spread, cream butter until soft and add that—good on whole wheat crackers.

One last liver suggestion. Substitute ground liver for ground beef in stuffed peppers.

And that just about brings us to hot appetizers, or hors d'oeuvres if you like. Actually, if you are planning dinner, it makes no sense at all to have hot appetizers, as they are much more fun to eat, and people will, and then not eat your dinner. However, for a large party they are good, if expensive. They require either a hot plate-chafing dish type deal or many little kids to go running around offering things. I have been on both ends of this last method and I think it pleases everybody. There was a party here to raise money for Ecology Action East, and we had Swedish Meatballs and Sweet-Sour Soyballs and everybody was really turned on. I'm not kidding; every time I went up or downstairs I passed the place where the meatballs sat, and there would be people hovering thickly and saying things like, "Well, I don't know what they are but they're *good*," or, "They're really far out—kind of Chinese, but fantastic!" You may wonder why we had soyballs. Well, first, soybeans are much cheaper than meat. They are rather bland, but delicious in a spicy sauce. The meatballs, incidentally, were about two-thirds bread and one-third meat. Everybody liked them though. Anyhow, here's how we did both dishes.

SWEDISH MEATBALLS

Combine
    2 pounds ground beef
    1 to 2 cups wheat germ
    Few slices whole wheat bread (soaked in milk and crumbled)
    1 egg

> ¼ cup soy grits
> 1 minced onion
> ¼ teaspoon grated lemon rind
> A pinch of allspice or nutmeg, salt and pepper

Roll into little balls and roll the balls in flour. Brown the balls in hot melted butter or oil. When well browned, remove balls from pan.

Stir in

> 1 cup of water
> ½ cup of red wine

Add

> A little flour stirred with cold water for thickening

Toss in

> A little healthy broth powder and some Worcestershire sauce

Let this gravy cook until slightly thickened and there is no raw flour taste. Return the balls to the gravy and heat through. Just before serving, stir in

> 1 cup sour cream

Serve garnished with parsley.

VARIATION (SWEETISH MEATBALLS)

Make meatball mixture, omitting lemon and nutmeg, and adding

> ¼ teaspoon Worcestershire
> ½ teaspoon basil
> ¾ cup applesauce (unsweetened)

Brown as above, but for sauce, use a mixture of

> 1⅓ cup tomato puree
> ⅔ cup water
> ⅓ tablespoon honey
> a fleck of cinnamon or cloves

These may be cooked on top of the stove but are better baked in the oven with the sauce poured over them. Bake for half an hour. Either recipe feeds 8-10.

Yet another phase of hot hors d'oeuvres is the filled thingie (for want of a better name). They are meat, fish, vegetable or what have you enclosed in a pastry of some sort. Every country has some version of these: Russia has pirozhki; China, egg rolls; India, samosas; France, crepes. This last is the only one I will include, mainly because they can be used as outsides for desserts, main dishes, what have you. It really doesn't make sense to me to have these as hors d'oeuvres. For a large group of people they get soggy; for small groups of people they spoil their appetite for supper. But do what you will.

LITTLE PANCAKES
(Crepes or pfannkuchen)

The recipe for these was given to me by Louise McGeorge, a friend from the town I grew up in. It's a good recipe. It is not difficult though it needs a little practice to be perfected, as does anything. It is both healthy and versatile.

Sift twice
    4 tablespoons buckwheat flour
Beat in a bowl
    6 eggs (yes—6)
Add the flour and
    2 tablespoons cold water
    ½ teaspoon salt
Beat all ingredients together till lumpless and the consistency of thin cream.

In a small heavy skillet, heat till it starts to bubble
    A small nubbin of butter
Shake the frying pan so it is buttered all over. Using ¼ cup measure, scoop out some batter and pour it into the pan, again shaking to spread batter as thin as possible. Cook for one minute on one side, flip over and cook for a minute on the other side. Stack finished pancakes on a heated plate, if possible. Fill and serve.

POSSIBLE FILLINGS:
As Hors d'oeuvres:
    Any curry: meat, poultry, seafood (Louise suggests crabmeat; see her recipe below).

Creamed anything: asparagus, chicken, shrimp, mushrooms.

Finely chopped ham browned with raisins, brown
sugar and lemon juice.

As Main Dish:

Any of the above, using larger pancakes and filling not
so finely chopped.

Dessert:

Custard, baked, turned out of the cup and spread on
pancake.

Alternately filled with cottage cheese, jam or cooked
apricots (you could add a bit of cinnamon to the
batter on these).

CURRY FILLING
(Louise McGeorge's crabmeat filling)

Melt in a saucepan or skillet
⅓ cup butter (or half butter, half oil)
Sauté therein (all finely chopped)
1 medium onion
1 apple
1 stalk celery
Now stir in
4 tablespoons whole wheat flour
Blend until smooth.
Add gradually, stirring
2½ cups broth of whatever kind of curry it is (chicken,
lamb, fish)
1 cup light cream (or evaporated milk)
Blend together
4 tablespoons cold water
1 teaspoon salt
1-4 teaspoons curry powder (or more if you like)
Combine the two mixtures. Simmer gently, stirring con-

stantly until thickened. Pour into a blender and whir a few moments. (If you don't have a blender, or if you do have one and don't want to wash it, skip it. It only makes the sauce much smoother.)

Return sauce to cooking pan. Add

    2½ cups plump crabmeat, lobster, chicken, mixed vegetables, or whatever, in bite-size pieces, cooked

Heat and serve, rolled up in crepes.

TIDBITS RUMAKI

This is a luxury dish.

Cut into bite-size pieces

    3 lobster tails or 6 or so chicken livers

Procure some toothpicks and skewer a lobster or liver piece on each along with:

    A water chestnut, sliced in half

Wrap around the two

    ½ slice bacon

Marinate for about 15 minutes in a mixture of

    ½ cup soy sauce

    2 tablespoons dry white wine

    Dash each ginger and sugar

Preheat broiler on high. Then turn heat down and arrange the rumaki thereon and broil close to the flame until the bacon is crisp, on low heat, about ten minutes. Although I have not tried it, I bet this would be delicious with sweetbreads. Incidentally, if you care about such things, be prepared to change the toothpicks before serving as they get rather weatherbeaten. And also this must be sizzling hot when you eat it. Its glamour fades when cold or lukewarm.

QUICHE

This too defies any classification as an appetizer, except

perhaps ease. It can be made in advance and served warm or cold. It is healthy and it is capable of vacuuming up leftovers in a truly remarkable and tasty manner. In short, it has my full recommendation.

Mix

    ½ cup each soy and rye flours

    1 cup raw wheat germ

    ¼ cup sesame seed

    ¼ cup oil

    Pinch of salt

    Cold water, to blend

You will be surprised how much water this drinks up before it becomes a good stiff dough which is then patted into one large or two smaller greased pie pans. It's because of the soy flour. Put the shells aside to chill while you prepare the filling.

First, slice rather thickly

    2 or 3 medium onions (it depends how much other stuff you're going to try to squeeze in. If you like, you can even use more)

Brown them well in as little oil as possible (or, use bacon fat, adding the crumbled bacon later on). Arrange the sautéed onions picturesquely in the shell.

Now scald

    1 cup milk

Remove from heat and stir in

    Grated or diced cheese—sharp, preferably, but a mixture is okay

Beat in

    3 to 4 eggs

    ⅓ cup powdered milk

    About a half teaspoon salt

    About ½ teaspoon basil

    Dash sea salt (see page 28)

    A little marjoram, sage, whatever you like

    Any leftover scraps of vegetables, meat, or fish, adding this last when the batter is smooth

Pour this into the shell and bake at 350° F. about 20 minutes to half an hour. When you take quiche out, sprinkle it all over with paprika. Chill, or leave warm or whatever until serving time.

meat

The supermarket variety of vegetable is fucked up, and so is the supermarket variety of meat and poultry, even more so. If one is going to eat meat (I do, vigorously) and be healthy about it (I try vigorously), organically raised livestock and chickens are the only answer. Not many people realize what is done to meat. First, most livestock is raised on pesticide-sprayed grain. This means that there are going to be high concentrations of it in their systems, higher than in the grain they ate, and then still higher in ours. Each animal eats many many times its weight in food in its lifetime, and long-lived pesticides, like DDT, are not passed through the system, but stored, usually in fat. Such a system is called a food chain. As described in *The Subversive Science:* "In the food web in which the herring gull is a scavenger in Lake Michigan, DDT, DDE and DDD concentrations in the bottom muds at 33-96 averaged 0.014 parts per million. In a shrimp they were 0.44 per million, more than ten times higher. Levels increased in fish to the range of a few per million (3.3 Alewife, 4.5 Chub, 5.6 Whitefish) another tenfold increase, and jumped in the omnivorous herring gull to 98.8 per million, twenty times higher still, and 7000 times as high as the mud." Rachel Carson tells of an obese man who went on a diet and promptly began to show symptoms of poisoning. DDT in the fat he was suddenly utilizing was being released in his bloodstream.

But this is not all that befalls an innocent cow and later not-so-innocent us. Many more people would become vegetarians if they realized that most animals raised for food are given an artificial sex hormone, stilbestrol, which puts cheap, quick weight on chickens or beef—all of it fat and water. Many, in addition, are treated with antibiotics either before or after slaughter—as a preventive against disease in the former case, as a preservative in the latter. They are also given tranquilizers periodically, but most often before being shipped to market to prevent their being nervous.

Nobody yet knows exactly what all these substances do to us. In experimental animals, stilbestrol has caused cancer of the breast, uterus, kidney, bladder, testes and blood-forming organs. We probably become resistant to antibiotics through constantly eating traces of them in meat, and should we need them, they might not affect us at all, or we might be overly sensitive to them. The same goes for tranquilizers. And no one knows what the combined effects of these chemicals are. We are the experimental animals.

There is a U.S. government publication entitled, "List of Chemical Compounds Authorized for use under USDA Poultry, Meat, Rabbit, and Egg Product Inspection Programs." The 1967 edition is 79 pages. The 1968 edition is 122 pages. Whoops!

It is for these reasons I would rather not eat nonorganic meat. The liver of any animal, be it calf, beef, pork, chicken, is incredibly high in the B Vitamins and Vitamin A and D and has a high quality of protein. Liver, then, theoretically, should be the most healthful of meats. But—every poison that enters the body must either be excreted rapidly in its original form or be slowly detoxified, made no longer poisonous, by the liver. This is true in any body—cow, chicken, pig, or human—and it means that if any of us consume poison, it congregates in our liver.

As usual, the poor people get the rawest end of an already raw deal. Poor in this country is practically synonymous with un- or less educated. Poor people have no idea of the shit being poured into their food and no chance of finding out, which at least the rest of us do. And even if they did, there's no escape for them. Healthful food is generally more expensive, even through a co-op. And poor people in a city are trapped therein with no chance to get out and "grow their own." And in the country, the poor are really poor and starving. They would be "lucky" to get the kind of diet that I and other middle-class people have rejected—just to keep them alive and at least not hungry.

What I'm saying here is: you can't get away from it. The answer is not really organic food, but revolution. Poisoned food is the symptom of a poisoned society.

It seems kind of idiotic, I know, to start in with Cooking and Eating after all that—but, survival right now. Practicality. So—if I haven't sold you yet on organic meat (every time I use that word I feel like putting quotation marks around it) let me give you some advice on ways to make regular cuts of meats a little less bad. First of all, buy lean meat as opposed to fatty or marbled meat. DDT is concentrated in fat. Trim all meat carefully and thoroughly, or cook whatever it is, chill it, and lift the fat from the top, where it will, of course, have risen. Obviously, this only works with some things, like soup or stew. Lean meat is tougher, but often flavorful and delicious with proper cooking. You can also have the butcher run it through one of his machines, the one which will make it come out looking as if teeth had scraped it. You can also tenderize it yourself —via marinades, rubbing certain things on it like the cut edge of a lemon, pineapple, or kiwi berry (more about this last later) or scoring it. You can score it by making cross cuts on its surface with a knife, like on a Virginia baked ham. Or by jabbing the knife through it repeatedly.

No matter what meat you get (especially if it's organic which is so expensive), you wish to make it taste its very tenderest, juiciest, most flavorful best. There is a cardinal rule, which, once learned, you will never forget, and which will help every scrap of meat, poultry, egg or cheese you cook and eat from then on. *High heat toughens protein.* A soufflé will toughen if baked at high heat, as will scrambled or even boiled eggs; cheese spread on crackers and put under the broiler to melt will become so incredibly horrible and chewy if the broiler is on high rather than somewhere between medium and low. Oriental food, both Chinese and Japanese, surely among the most delicious cuisines in the world, is based on this principle. The meat is diced or sliced small (necessary for consuming with chopsticks) and cooked quickly over medium heat. Most Chinese recipes that I have seen are followed by the admonition: "Do not exceed cooking time." So remember, and your protein food will be much the better for low heat—not only in taste but in nutrients as well.

SUKIYAKI

This recipe is the perfect example of how completely successful the Oriental school of cooking is. It was given to me by Ann Tsubota, who makes pottery along with Big Diane and gave us ten ceramic glasses, scalloped in deep brown, when we first moved in.

Slice very thin

> 2 pounds top sirloin (this is much easier to do if the meat is frozen)

Brown the meat in a large skillet using no oil. Add

> Enough water to just cover the meat
>
> 1 medium-large bottle of Kikkoman shoyu (soy sauce)
>
> 3 tablespoons raw sugar
>
> 2 tablespoons sherry

The sauce should taste slightly sweet.

Add enough of the following vegetables to fill pan

> 1 pound fresh washed spinach
>
> 1 cup mushrooms, sliced
>
> 2 onions, sliced
>
> 2½ cups bean sprouts
>
> 3 bunches scallions, cut in 2-inch lengths
>
> 1 or 2 squares tofu (bean curd) diced—available in Chinatown
>
> 2 carrots sliced

It is easier if you arrange all these vegetables on a platter beforehand. At any rate, don't add all the vegetables in one fell swoop. You can make another batch later. Cook quickly—no more than fifteen minutes over medium heat at the most. Try to keep each vegetable separate during cooking. To serve: each person should have three bowls, a sukiyaki bowl, a rice bowl, and a bowl with a raw beaten egg in it. Each person dips a piece of sukiyaki in the egg and scarfs it down. Ann thinks this was originally done to cool the food. Pour the sauce over the rice. This will feed a surprising number of people and the amount of vegetables can be increased.

Although Ann does not do this, some Japanese restaurants add a meatball or two per skillet of sukiyaki. This is practical, because there are some parts of a sirloin steak that are too fatty and tough to work successfully sliced.

TO MAKE MEAT BALLS FOR SUKIYAKI:
Grind all the scrips and scraps of fatty sirloin, or bits too little to make a slice. If there's an amount of any size, add an egg. Mix well and add soy grits, enough to make it a meatballable texture. Brown with the slices of beef. And there you are!

This next recipe is completely different from the preceding but it is really good, especially, it seems to me, on cold nights, accompanied by mashed potatoes. Incidentally, I was asked to revise some of the book by Simon and Schuster—put in more about us and fewer recipes. So you know that all the recipes that made it thus far are my (or our) very, very, very favorites.

SWISS STEAK

Any rather toughish meat responds to this treatment.
Cut into pieces, serving-size ones
    2 pounds round steak
Dredge the pieces in
    Cornmeal and whole wheat flour seasoned with salt
        and pepper
Brown the pieces in
    Oil

Remove to another plate, and brown in the same pan
> Several onions, sliced

When brown, add the steak strips and
> 2 to 3 cups canned whole tomatoes, mushed with a fork, or fresh peeled ones, cut up
>
> 1 tablespoon raw sugar
>
> A few good dashes of Worcestershire sauce
>
> ¼ cup good hearty red wine
>
> ½ teaspoon each celery seed and basil

Simmer until tender over a very, very low heat, somewhere around an hour and a half, covered tightly and stirring every once in a while. If you like, add in the last fifteen minutes
> ½ cup sliced mushrooms

This humble and peasanty dish is really fine. It should, as said earlier, be served with potatoes (mashed with skin) but brown rice or bread are good too, to sop up the delicious gravy.

VARIATION: Omit the tomatoes and sugar and spices, using instead more onions, half a clove garlic and ½ cup each boiling beef broth or consommé, red or white wine. This excellent variation is a less earthy dish, more subtle and light.

CHINA STEW

This is very rich, fragrant and strong-flavored. From Miss Kay, a lady I've known all my life.

In
> Bacon fat

Brown well
> 2 pounds beef chuck, cut for stew

Cook for about five minutes, and then add
> 2 cups water

Let it boil down a little and then add
> ½ cup soy sauce and 1 star anise, whole

Cook till very tender over low heat 1½ hours. Thicken with
> 3 teaspoons cornstarch; remove anise

Serve with brown rice.

Next we come to ground meat, always the cheapest, even (comparatively speaking) amongst organic meat. Its amorphous nature makes it fair game for sneaking in various healthful things. A healthful meat loaf may be had by changing your favorite meat loaf recipe (or rather, since no one *Really* likes meat loaf, the one you least dislike). Use soy grits instead of bread crumbs to bind, or use whole-grain bread crumbs and add a few tablespoons each of nutritional yeast, wheat germ and milk powder.

GENIE'S MOTHER'S HOMEMADE CHILI

Genie Reese is a long-time friend of Crispin's from Texas (of course: Chili—Texas) and shorter-time friend of mine in New York. This recipe is thick and opulently spicy. Exact quantities for spices cannot be given for it is strictly to taste. Genie, who spent one whole afternoon compiling all her favorite recipes for this collection, writes of it, "This used to be an all-day process. We would all go to this fantastic spice shop to buy the ingredients for it."

Render the fat from suet in a skillet and remove the piece of suet afterwards.

Rendering, in case you don't know, is drawing the fat from the meat by cooking it. Now this fat gives the chili a delicious flavor, but it also has all the DDT, so you have to decide. A few tablespoons of olive oil can be used if you vote against it.
Now add

> About 3 pounds ground beef, good quality (Crispin, who also considers himself somewhat an authority on Mexican food, having spent 9 months in a Mexican jail, would advise chopping finely rather than grinding)

Now add

> Lots of black pepper and salt

Cook till grainy and brown. Now the seasonings

> 2 cloves of garlic, whole
> 1 hot black chili pepper, whole

Ground cumin seed, chili pepper, black chili pepper,
    oregano
Put
    3 cans tomato paste
    3 cans water
in the pan. Bring to a boil, reduce heat and simmer about 45
minutes or until done. Serve over real imported Mexican chili
beans. The beans must be soaked overnight and simmered till
tender in a large pot with a piece of salt pork or bacon meat. 4½
pounds of beans will neatly fit this recipe of chili.

ALTERNATE AND HEALTHIER COOKING VERSION:

Brown the beef as directed above, add the spices and refrigerate overnight. In the morning, stir in 2 cans tomato paste
but no water, or only a little bit. Heat through and serve.

TAMALE PIE

This sounds much nicer by its Spanish name, *maíz con
carne molida de cazuela*. Whatever you care to call it, it's good
and pretty to look at too, all little flecks of yellow and green
and red, especially nice in a brown pottery casserole such as
Big Diane has made.

FILLING:

Sauté
    1 green and 1 red pepper, diced (no difference except
        for color—although the red has more Vitamin C)
    2 to 3 onions, chopped
    A clove of garlic
    ½ teaspoon cumin seeds
In
    As little oil as possible—about 2 tablespoons olive oil
        is nice
Add
    1½ pounds ground fairly lean meat, part beef and part
        pork, or all beef or part liver and part heart and
        part beef—whatever

Brown the meat well, over low to medium heat, turning occasionally. Drain any excess-seeming fat, and stir in

> 2 tablespoons whole wheat flour, to pull it together
> 2-4 tablespoons nutritional yeast

Stir well, and add

> As many chopped, pitted olives as you can afford, at least ¼ cup
> 2½-3 cups tomatoes, canned or fresh peeled and chopped
> chili powder to taste (our taste is about 3 tablespoons)
> Few vigorous dashes Tabasco or similar hot pepper preparation
> 1 teaspoon salt, large pinch freshly ground black pepper
> 2 cups corn, canned or cooked and cut from the cob

Let this sit while you prepare the crust, which is not really a crusty crust at all, but cornmeal mush, or polenta.

CRUST:

Bring to a boil

> 2 cups water

While it is being brought to a boil, stir together until lumpless in this order

> 1 cup cornmeal
> ½ cup milk powder
> 1 cup *cold* water

Now add this to the boiling water and stirring constantly (get someone to help you do this, it's harrowing, and use a heavy pot), cook over low heat about fifteen minutes. After about ten minutes, great large science-fiction-type bubbles will begin to erupt and splosh. Keep on stirring, undaunted. After the cornmeal has cooked for fifteen or twenty minutes and thickened considerably, line a well-greased casserole with it. Pour or spoon or ladle or dip the meat-corn-tomato stuff into it.

> Top with
>> Sharp grated cheddar or monterey jack cheese, about 1 cup

Bake at 325° F. for about a half hour and serve immediately with a crisp green salad or green vegetable like broccoli.

You may have wondered at the weird assortment of organ meats I advise instead of plain old ground beef. Well, the reason is that if people don't like plain liver, for example, which is very good for them, the flavor of it in such a dish is but mildly discernible. Conversely, if people do like liver, there will be some taste of it, but it will not be nearly so expensive as if it were 100 per cent liver. You see? So everybody winds up happy. It's just a question of putting it in the right terms.

You may wonder, in addition, how to grind organ meats, since, if you order organic stuff, it will come whole. Well, the answer is simple—get a meat grinder. They are very cheap, about two dollars (the hand ones), and can be used for all kinds of things: making pâtés and spreads, grinding organ meats and in case you some day become a vegetarian, soy beans and lentils in recipes such as Sweet-Sour Soy Balls. They are also kind of fun to operate, in a perverse sort of way. At least I like to grind stuff (within reason). At any rate, I am opposed to superfluous possessions and I really think this is not one. Incidentally, if someone gives you an old-fashioned coffee grinder (as happened to us) and you drink only instant coffee or none at all (as we do) it can be useful as more than just a wall decoration—they really are quite pretty and unusual looking. Ours, besides being a strange shape that prompts everyone to say "What *is* that?" has, for some reason I do not know, the brand name "Zassenhaus" under a picture of a sphinx with an umbrella over its shoulder. They can grind whole grains into grits to then be cooked as porridge or added to things. Of course, it is obvious after you think about it that this would work, but we never thought about it. It took one of the neighborhood kids, Junior, fooling around on a rainy day with it, to discover it. Although I would still define the coffee grinder as superfluous (not something to carry with you in case you get lost in the woods), it is at least less superfluous if used to grind grains into grits. Actually this whole paragraph has been rather superfluous, speaking of superfluous things!

The Middle Eastern restaurant that prompted us to figure out how to make hommos prompted us to do this next. It has come out completely different but really good all the same.

That restaurant is great: a big clean plain room with meat-brown curtains tied back on the front window and a rather rowdy flashing light saying Shish Kebab, the only rowdy part about it. A sign says HOME-STYLE COOKING, EAT HERE AND FEEL AT HOME. A family owns and operates it and they obviously dig doing it. On slow nights, the family, including a grizzled and venerable Arab who is clearly at the top, comes out and takes over a table in the dining room chopping carrots and talking in loud, foreign voices. At busier times, they stay closed in the kitchen except the mother and the teen-age kids who scurry around doing things. The jukebox, which plays only busy nights, alternates Middle Eastern music, which, in case you haven't heard any, is very whiney to the Western ear, and soul music (no doubt very whiney to the Eastern ear). Perhaps the best part (except the food) is the bathroom which, like almost all restaurant bathrooms in New York City, has a little sign saying ALL EMPLOYEES MUST WASH HANDS BEFORE LEAVING THIS ROOM, BY ORDER OF THE CITY COMMISSIONER OF HEALTH—and there is no sink! It's beautiful. (For those of you who are curious, the sink is right outside.)

But the food! It's just standard Middle Eastern food, I guess: stuffed grape leaves, lamb everything—with okra, with spinach, with squash—shish kebab, and baklava, remarkable honey-soaked pastries for dessert. But it's so good! It comes to the table steaming hot, in large, pretty-looking portions (except for stuffed tripe, which is the ugliest thing you ever saw, like two old leather bags—but that's how tripe is, and it really tastes good if you can get over its appearance). At any rate, it's a very nice place, and cheap too. I was taken to dinner there by Cheryl Hess, a friend of ours, in celebration of the publication of this book. You should see some of the mistakes I make—maybe they should be left in. Proofreading back a few weeks ago, I found I had typed brain the onion, as opposed to brown the onion. I must have been rather tired that night, as I must have been wide awake when I wrote, add the celery hopped up. At any rate (seems I've heard that somewhere before), here's the recipe—a revised version of:

MID-EAST ORIENTAL STUFFED EGGPLANT

Again you need a meat grinder. Although lamb is usually used herein, there's no reason why you shouldn't substitute something else once in a while.

Grind (or have it ground)

    1 pound lean lamb

Next, in

    1 cup water

Soak

    1 cup bulgar wheat (available at Pete's or any Health Food or Middle Eastern food store)

Mix the two together, after the wheat and the water have soaked half an hour. Add and mix

    1 large onion, finely chopped

    1 teaspoon salt

    ½ teaspoon cinnamon

    Allspice, clove—vigorous dash each

    1 grind of pepper

If you have time, put through the meat grinder again, if not, leave it as is. Now, take

    2 large beautiful eggplants

After fondling them, slice crosswise in fairly thick slices, leaving peel on. Cut out the center of each slice, leaving a ring of eggplant. A small round cooky cutter works efficiently for this. Now, add to the stuffing mixture

    3-4 tablespoons melted butter

Place the eggplant rings in a shallow, flat, greased casserole. Stuff each ring well and cover the casserole tightly. Bake, covered in preheated oven at 325° F. for 35 minutes. Remove cover and sprinkle over the rings

    1 can tomatoes, squished, and their juice, or the same amount of fresh peeled tomatoes

Uncover and cook ten minutes longer. Serve immediately.

While I'm at it, I might as well give you another Middle Eastern recipe, that of Kibbe (also spelled Kibbee and Kibbeh). This is similar to the above but is drier and minus the eggplant and tomato treatment. It is really good, better than it sounds, and is certainly simpler to prepare than Stuffed Eggplant. It is good cold, too, in lunchboxes.

KIBBE

Make the same filling as for Mid-East Oriental Stuffed Eggplant using 2 pounds of lamb, 1 cup bulgar and not quite double the spices. 1 onion will suffice. Grind twice, as above, and add ice water, if need be, to make the mixture moist and soft. You won't need very much.

Pat the mixture into a greased shallow square pan, and with a knife, cut it into diamonds or squares, as you might brownies, *before* baking. Dot the surface liberally with butter, say about half a stick or four tablespoons, and sprinkle well with pine nuts. These are expensive but you don't need very many. Bake at 375° F. for about an hour, till golden and slightly crusty. Lift out each section and serve.

They're good cold and hold together well for lunch bags, etc. Sometimes I use ¾ cup bulgar and ¼ cup wheat germ and the results have been pretty good.

Lamb chops, for some reason, respond incredibly well to being sautéed with nothing more than butter and soy sauce. This is Michael's trick. Michael worked his way through college cooking and is very good at it. In addition, he has practiced quantity cooking, a useful occupation around here. He taught me that 1) large groups of people always eat less than you think they will and 2) that they like gelatin salads, and 3) that any leftover is good with cheese melted over it. I don't know if I agree with that last, but he and Ronnie sure practice it. Their breakfasts are an exotic combination of leftover rice heated with fish, nuts, seeds, raisins, and, of course, cheese. They're usually good. Their dinners, perhaps 60 percent of the time, are an equally exotic mixture based on shrimp and soy sauce, the recipe for which follows later. At any rate, they are both good cooks.

Stewing lamb, to my way of thinking, is more or less a waste of time, as is stewing veal. These meats are tender and succulent and young and are more delicious prepared in other ways. Tough beef (and mutton too, I would think, though I've never had the occasion to try any) are the meats to stew. Long, slow cooking brings out the best in them; they become ten-der*er* and more flavorful. Almost any meat can be improved or at least varied by being marinated awhile. Marinades also serve the purpose of tenderizing certain meats, if long enough bathed therein. Shashlik or shish kebab are both lamb dishes, marinated in either sweet or savory concoctions and threaded on skewers and broiled. The skewers, mind, are strictly for show. You can easily do without them.

SAVORY MARINADE

Mix together
    1 cup of oil, healthy (olive is nice, but so expensive)
    ½-1 cup cider or wine vinegar
    1 teaspoon-2 tablespoons honey
    Salt and pepper to taste
    ½ teaspoon or more dry mustard and rosemary

SWEET MARINADE

Follow the above, omitting mustard and adding fruit juice to replace part of the vinegar, or just adding it. Orange juice, pineapple juice, berry juices fresh or from concentrates can all be used with success. Ginger, cinnamon, allspice and clove may be added to a sweet marinade; Tabasco sauce, tomato juice, basil and any other herb can be added to the Savory.

Wine, white or red, or sherry can be added with beneficial results to either. At any rate, if shashlik is what you want to make, marinate lamb in Savory Marinade overnight, or at least 2 hours, adding mushroom caps and green pepper slices for the last half hour. Thread the above, with quarters of ripe tomatoes and onions, on skewers, or just sprinkle all of these on a greased broiler and broil under medium heat for about ten minutes, close to flame, turning occasionally. Shish kebab sits overnight in a Sweet Marinade, to be joined en brochette with pineapple chunks, cherries, and any vegetable used in shashlik.

And now we come to pork. Whether it should be included in a book on healthy foods I really don't know. So many people and tribes consider it unhealthy, the Jews and Muslims for instance. Part of this, of course, stems from the fact that pigs carry trichinosis, a tapeworm of some sort. This can be killed easily by simply cooking all pork well, but some people feel that anything that can even carry a tapeworm must be bad. And some people also think that pig meat is just too fatty. Myself, I don't know. I don't like the taste of pork as well as some other meats, but it is good combined with certain things, fruit in one recipe, and a spicy Chinese vegetable sauce in another.

No one knows where this first recipe came from. It was lying in a drawer, loose, with a lot of other recipes. It sounded good to me and I suggested Crispin make it one night when he was cooking. He did, and it was really fine. We had thought it was Big Diane's recipe (it looked like her handwriting) but it wasn't. So—it's a mystery, but truly delicious and here it is.

APPLE-GLAZED PORK LOIN

Into
> A pork loin—about 4 pounds

Rub
> 1 tablespoon flour

1 tablespoon dry mustard
1 teaspoon salt
¼ teaspoon pepper

Put in a shallow roasting pan. Bake at 325° F. for an hour, remove and pour over the roast

2 cups applesauce
1 teaspoon cinnamon
½ tablespoon molasses
¼ cup raw sugar
Dash allspice, ginger

Return to the oven. Figure out how long it needs to be in there. Thorough cooking requires 40 minutes a pound, including that first hour. Baste often while cooking.

During the last half hour, cover, surround roast with

2 cups apples, tart, cored, sliced but not peeled

Sprinkle the apples with

More raw sugar—about ¼ cup and molasses
About ½ teaspoon cinnamon and ginger

Serve with sweet potatoes. This is really good and also pretty to look at, kind of cover of McCall's-y.

This next recipe is entirely different. It is a combination of several favorites of mine, put together for the celebration of two friends' anniversary—Ray and Genie (Genie of Chili fame among others). Ray and Genie and Crispin and Shelley and I sat around eating and eating and eating like swine, nobody saying anything except Ray going, occasionally, "My *God*, Crescent, my *God*." That was a dinner. We had eggrolls (home-made—space does not permit the recipe here), rice, cake, watermelon sherbet, fruit cup and the dish below.

CHINESE PORK AND VEGETABLES

Soak in warm water for about half an hour
12 or so dried black Chinese mushrooms

Drain, saving ½ cup of the mushroom water. Put the mushrooms aside.

Mix the mushroom water with

    2 tablespoons soy sauce

    1½ tablespoons cornstarch

    1 tablespoon sherry

Set aside. Over

    1¼ pound pork shoulder, diced or cut in strips (not ground) pour

    3 tablespoons soy sauce

    1 tablespoon honey or raw sugar

    1 teaspoon salt

    ¼ teaspoon ground white pepper

Let this stand while you sauté in about 1 tablespoon hot oil (preferably peanut)

    1½ cloves garlic, ground

    3 or 4 slices fresh ginger root, chopped

Sauté for about two minutes. The smell is very Chinesey at this point. Ginger and garlic are the base for many Chinese stir-fry dishes. Now add

    1 small can water chestnuts, sliced

    1 cup snow peas (in pods, of course)

    3 bamboo shoots, sliced along the grain

    5 stalks Chinese celery, bok choy, sliced in about 1-inch pieces (don't use the leafy green part which is bitter)

Add the soaked mushrooms, also sliced, and cook, stirring, five minutes (this is what is meant by stir-fry). *It is essential with Chinese foods that you cook exactly as many minutes as the recipe says.* Okay, now. Remove these vegetables from the pan (a large one) and set aside.

Add

    Another 2 tablespoons oil

Heat, and add the pork. Cook, stirring constantly, five minutes.

Add the first vegetable mixture and

    2 squares tofu (bean curd), diced

    1 cup or a bit less bean sprouts

Add the cornstarch mixture and cook, stirring constantly five minutes. Serve immediately, stirring in if you like, to make it go farther

> 1 head lettuce, chopped finely

This also adds a nice texture. Top with toasted blanched almonds and serve with brown rice.

This recipe may also be used with beef. One last word about this one: the ginger flavor in it is rather pronounced and you may wish to tone it down a bit. Also you should get everything diced before you start.

Just one more pork recipe, and that for a delicious all-American-tasting ham.

HAM BAKED IN CIDER AND HONEY

Remove any rind and score the fat in a diamond on

> 1 cooked ham, 4 pounds

Stud with cloves and put the ham in a roasting pan.
In a large saucepan bring to a boil

> 1 cup water
> 2 tablespoons honey
> 4 cups apple cider
> 1 onion, quartered
> ½ cinnamon stick

Boil ten minutes. Remove the cinnamon stick. Strain, and pour over the ham. Bake at 375°F. for about fifteen minutes per pound.

Remove from the roasting pan. Strain the pan juices. Combine them with

> 1 tablespoon lemon juice
> 2 tablespoons whole wheat flour
> Enough cider to make 2 cups juice

Cook, stirring constantly, until thickened and no raw flour taste remains, a bit over 5 minutes. Serve this sauce on the ham.

organ meats

And now, having laid on you some of my very favorite more conventional meat recipes, we turn to organ meats. Organ meats are, simply, the organs as opposed to the flesh of the animals we eat: liver, thymus gland, brain, kidney—all organs. Many are extraordinarily healthy, like liver, and many are extraordinarily good, like sweetbreads (the thymus). Nearly all are comparatively cheap, having no bone and little fat or waste. Poor people and gourmets have long known the value of organ meats. But the vast majority (the silent one, you know) of us, while gladly sinking out teeth into a bloody rare roast or steak, pale at the thought of eating something's liver or heart or kidney or brain. This is our white middle-class heritage—we never grew up eating any of these things, number one, and number two, more important, most of us don't like to be reminded that we eat real animals, that we eat cow and not beef, pig and not pork. Animal organ names correspond uncomfortably enough with our own organ names. So without thinking of it, we just kind of go yeech when someone mentions eating such things.

This was, and still is, a little true with me. A year ago, I *never* would have eaten an animal's heart, say. But living here, I grew to realize that many things that I did were just irrational, and further, I should try and change those things. It doesn't make sense to eat one part of an animal and categorically refuse to even try another.

I tackled the problem head on. I *would* cook organ meats, and I would like them. I managed to cook them and, finally, to eat them. I found, as with other foods, some kinds I liked and others I didn't. The first one I tried was heart. It was a good first choice although it looked like what it is—heart, complete with valves along the edge, and promised to be difficult to handle. Really, handling is the hardest part. (That presupposes that you, like me, are fucked up.) We cubed the heart, marinated it and broiled it with fresh pineapple, tomatoes, mushrooms, onions, and green peppers. Although anything probably would be delicious prepared this way, this seemed especially so. The heart of young animals (we used calf's heart) is very tender and tastes like the very finest, best-quality beef. It has little or none of that soft texture which people may find objectionable, myself included—though less and less all the time. Besides being shish-kebabed, heart can also be ground and used in any recipe calling for ground beef. Heart is more nutritious, having a higher protein level. It can be stuffed—this is the most common way of preparing it—and baked slowly to succulent perfection. Older and hence tougher heart responds well when prepared in this way. The only difficulty is—it arrives at the table looking like Stuffed Heart.

My next choice, regarding my organ meat liberation, was sweetbreads. These are the thymus gland, located in the chest of young animals. A gland in the throat is also sometimes sold as sweetbreads. Sweetbreads are rather expensive and very delicate in flavor, a little like chicken, quite soft in texture, and the favorite of gourmets around the world. They, too, were good, but after preparing them in a casserole with mushrooms, I realized—and this should be axiomatic for persons cooking organ meats—they need to be combined with something crisp, like water chestnuts or celery, to contrast with their soft, limp insides. This is also true of brains, too often coupled with equally squishy scrambled eggs. So I worked out some appropriate recipes.

I was really looking forward to my next sally forth—liver. I was convinced I'd like it. I *had* to. Liver is the healthiest thing in the world, I do believe. It contains Vitamins A and C as well as the B's. A slice of it weighing 3½ ounces has from 26 to 32 grams of protein, depending on what animal it comes from, as opposed to 19 grams in the same amount of roast beef. But all this healthiness takes place only in organic liver, because, as mentioned earlier, the liver detoxifies the body, making harmless the poisons therein, so if the body has consumed poisons, they will collect in the liver awaiting detoxification. So, we ordered a few pounds of organic liver from the Co-op. I'll tell you, I was really looking forward to it. Liver was the one organ meat I'd had before going on my spree. I hadn't liked it. But, I decided, it was because I could *taste* all those poisons in it. I was going to *love* organic liver. To make a long story short, I didn't, I really didn't.

Liver, there is no denying, has a very strong pervasive flavor. I think it is the iron in it which some people like. The Dianes, both of them, do. Crispin does. Lots of people do. Me, I keep trying, choking it down persistently. Perhaps I am a dreamer, but I am sure *someday* I will like it. Actually, the conflict between liver and myself seems to have lessened considerably already. I had some last night—cut into little pieces, breaded well, first in whole wheat flour, then egg, then wheat germ. I fried it to a golden crispness, which, since I like crisp things, took my mind off its being liver. I then drowned it in a pungent sauce. I will fool around until I find the perfect ways to make liver taste good. Here are a couple of ways.

CRISP LIVER

In flour, dredge one large but very thin slice of liver per person. Dip the floured slices first in a beaten egg, then in wheat germ. Fry in hot oil until golden brown and crisp or broil until same. Serve plain or in any of the following sauces:

CHINESE SWEET SOUR LIVER—Cut liver into small squares and bread and brown as above. Remove from pan. In the same pan, heat 1½ cups pineapple juice and a dozen pearl onions, halved. Cook covered for ten minutes. Blend together one cup of tomato puree, one cup pineapple juice, 2 tablespoons soy sauce, ¾ cup mild vinegar, heaping ½ cup cornstarch. Add to sauce in pan and stir until thick and clear. Pour over liver.

SWISS STYLE LIVER—Make Swiss steak sauce as directed on page 54, sauté liver as above, and add it to the cooked sauce.

EASY SAUCE FOR LIVER—2 parts lemon juice, 1 part honey.

ORIENTAL LIVER

Mix together
    ¼ cup sherry
    2 tablespoons soy sauce
    ½ to 1 teaspoon mild honey
    2 tablespoons cornstarch
    2 tablespoons water
Marinate in this a few minutes
    2 pounds calves' liver cut in thin matchstick strips
Heat
    ¼ cup oil
Sauté
    1 clove minced garlic and a slice of ginger (optional)
Add the liver and sauté, stirring often, for 3 minutes.
Mix in
    ½ cup sliced scallions or green onions
    ½ cup water chestnuts, chopped fairly small (in quarters or so)
    ½ cup bean sprouts
Cook over low heat another three minutes, season with salt and pepper and serve.

LIVER AND HEART SHASHLIK

Make a marinade of
    ½ cup lemon juice

¼ cup oil
1 teaspoon black pepper
1 hot dried pepper, crushed
1 bay leaf
1 tablespoon parsley
Marinate in this overnight
1½ pounds calves liver, deveined and cubed
1 calf's heart, trimmed

Next day, skewer meat and broil till done. Serve with a hot tomato sauce seasoned with chili powder, onions, garlic, and salt. Serves 6.

HEART

The marinade we used for the heart shish kebab was a basic sweet marinade, made with orange juice and sherry and oil and vinegar and seasoned with a little cinnamon, allspice and rosemary. The heart we used was calf, which is very tender and comparatively costly. But the heart of any young animal would be fine, a lamb heart for example. It was then broiled quickly under medium heat for a few minutes, along with the aforementioned fruit and vegetables: fresh pineapple, tomatoes, mushrooms, onions and green pepper. Beef hearts seem to be tenderer if served cold, sliced. They slice well and are an excellent meat for sandwiches.

HEART IN SURPRISING SAUCE

Use
½ beef heart

Prepare it by cutting off valves and tubes and then cubing it as for stew. Cut it as much as possible across the grain.

Put it in a large casserole and cover it with
4 cups (1 quart) tomatoes, canned, or fresh peeled and chopped

Season with
> 1½ teaspoons salt
> ½ teaspoon fresh ground black pepper
> 2 teaspoons honey
> ½ bay leaf
> 1 teaspoon basil

Mix in
> 1½ cups pitted or unpitted dried prunes

Now if you leave them unpitted, be sure to warn everyone. Stewed prunes may also be used. Cover very tightly and simmer over low, low heat until tender—perhaps four hours. Or bake at 200°F. for the same period of time, or a bit longer. If it dries out, add a little beef or heart stock or vegetable cooking water or tomato juice. Twenty minutes before eating, add
> 2 green peppers, seeded and chopped
> 1-2 onions, quartered, or eighthed, if large
> 2 potatoes, sliced, with skin on
> 1-2 stalks of broccoli, in large slices

Cover and turn the heat up slightly. Simmer ten or fifteen minutes, until the vegetables are cooked but not mushy. Serve steaming hot over millet.

HEART WITH HORSERADISH SAUCE

Prepare
> ½ beef heart

by cutting off fat and larger tubes. Wait till it's cooked, however, to complete trimming. It will be easier then. Place in a pot, cover with water, add a tablespoon or two of vinegar, and simmer for about two hours. The stock is not used in this recipe, but it definitely should be saved and used later in various things. It is most flavorful. In fact, I usually cook up a few beef bones in it (under the treatment described in *Stock,* page 30) and make some sort of soup the next day. I remove the heart before adding the bones, however, so it will not surrender all its flavor to the broth.

Let the heart cool at room temperature but do not chill.

When it is quite cool, slice it. You will be amazed at how easily it slices. Arrange the slices neatly on a platter and make the following sauce. Mix together

> ½ cup sour cream
> ½ teaspoon-1 tablespoon prepared horseradish (this depends on how hot you like it)
> 1 tablespoon onion, finely chopped

Spoon this sauce over the heart slices, sprinkle with parsley and paprika, and serve. It's an excellent summer dish, good with tomatoes sprinkled with sweet basil.

SWEETBREADS

Sweetbreads are the thymus gland, and the thymus gland, according to Webster's New World Dictionary of the American language, is "a ductless, glandlike body, of undetermined function, situated in the upper thorax near the throat: it is most prominent at puberty, after which it disappears or becomes vestigial." At any rate, they are high in protein and various vitamins, expensive (as organ meats go—$1.50 a pound in New York) and really delicious, the only organ meat (with the exception of heart) which I eat without reservation in large, happy bites. Precooking depletes them of some of their vitamins, which dissolve into their cooking water. However, if all the cooking water is then used in the recipe this is no problem, and the sweetbreads are easily handled and nutritious, like in this first recipe, which combines soft with crunchy textures.

CHINESE SWEETBREADS AND ALMONDS

Precook

> 1½ pounds sweetbreads

by dropping into 1½ cups simmering water to which ½ teaspoon salt and 1 tablespoon of either vinegar or lemon juice has been added. Cool the sweetbreads slightly and de-membrane them—the larger membranes.

Reserve the cooking water and simmer in it

> 1 or 2 pieces of chicken

which you are using for other things. You just need it here to give the broth a chickeny flavor. If this step seems wasteful to you, I suppose you could add some chicken broth powder to the sweetbreads' liquor, but the chicken flavor is definitely necessary for the success of this dish. Refrigerate both sweetbreads and broth until ready to use.

Heat

> 3 tablespoons oil

Sauté in it for two minutes, stirring constantly

> 1 or 2 onions, eighthed
>
> ½ pound fresh snow peas
>
> 1 cup canned button mushrooms
>
> 1 cup sliced water chestnuts

Add the mushroom and water chestnut waters from the cans to the chicken-sweetbread broth and heat well. Measure out 2½ cups of it and add to the vegetables after they have cooked their 2 minutes. Also add

> The prepared sweetbreads (which have been pulled into bite-size pieces)
>
> 1½ teaspoons salt, ½ teaspoon black pepper
>
> 3-4 tablespoons soy sauce

Cook, covered tightly, 5 minutes. Meanwhile, mix together

> 2½ tablespoons cornstarch
>
> 4 tablespoons water

After five minutes stir this mixture into the sweetbreads and vegetables. Stir until thickened and add

> 1 cup blanched toasted almonds

Serve immediately, steaming hot, over rice. Use the almond blanching water to cook rice with.

KIDNEYS

Last but not least we come to kidneys. These highly nutritious organs are held in somewhat lower repute than most of the other "variety meats" by almost everybody except a few enlightened gourmets and, of course, poor people. Because, boy, kidneys sure are cheap. You can get a pound of them for forty cents in New York City. And they're incredibly good for you: 3½ ounces of them more than double the amount of protein in a pork chop. An average-size chop has 16 grams of proteins and the same weight of kidneys, 33! In addition, they have high amounts of iron and calcium and Vitamin A and the B Vitamins and the mysterious and protective anti-stress factor (read Adelle Davis on that one). So, along with liver, they are the most nutritious of meats. And, they taste good too! They don't have much of that soft squishy organ-meat texture and though they taste a bit liver-like they are not nearly as strong in flavor. And yet, on most farms, kidneys are thrown out if the animal is home butchered, and most people in the city won't eat them. The reason is obvious: kidneys make piss. They smell strongly of ammonia, and—again—they make piss. At least to the uneducated eye (or nose). But listen to what Adelle Davis says about kidneys in *Let's Cook It Right*:

> Around the outer layer, or cortex, of a kidney are several million tiny knots of capillaries. The walls of these capillaries in a single kidney, if laid flat, are estimated to cover more than a square mile. Through this tremendous surface the force of the blood pressure pushes blood plasma chemically identical to the juices of meats universally thought delicious. The blood plasma flows through tiny tubes surrounding the knots of capillaries into connecting tissue, which is white. It is only when the plasma reaches this white tissue it takes on the composition of urine. In preparing kidneys, therefore, let no water touch them until the white tissue is snipped away with the kitchen scissors.
>
> When kidneys are cooked at too high temperature or overcooked, an odor of ammonia can be detected. Since ammonia occurs in urine, an untrained person assumes that the odor of improperly cooked kidney proves that the meat is saturated with urine. All proteins and the products into which used proteins are

changed contain nitrogen. Much nitrogen is converted by enzymes in the kidney into ammonia which readily dissolves in water; in this way nitrogen no longer needed by the body can be thrown off. Heat accelerates enzyme action, or the production of ammonia, and also causes ammonia to evaporate. Although this odor does not indicate that urine is in the kidney tissues, a little vinegar should be added to neutralize the ammonia.

So you see, we have here another irrational hang-up. I think you'll find kidneys are not difficult at all—if you try them.

The house, for the most part, was annoyed that I was making kidneys. Big Diane and Susan like them, but Freddy bitched and Mike and Ronnie went out for dinner, Michael saying petulantly and semi-seriously even, "Well, if you're going to have *that*, I'm *leaving!*" though he was anyhow. Everyone else (myself included) remained silently dubious. But then I set them down on the table. Delicious-smelling steam issued from the cast-iron pot. Freshly shelled green peas, stewed tomatoes, onions, corn, mushrooms, red wine, basil, rosemary and bay leaf made a richly seasoned and colorful gravy everyone agreed to try, it looked so pretty. And they did. And came back for second and third helpings. And when Mike and Ronnie came back (Mike, no doubt, ready to make some snide remark about the leftovers—he and I quite literally treat each other as brother and sister, as of late) there was not a scrap left.

KIDNEY STEW

The only hassle is cutting out the connective tissue of the kidneys. As Adelle Davis suggests, snipping them with a scissors is easiest. It is, however, tedious and time-consuming work, even though it's not necessary to get every single scrap of white tissue, so you should get someone to help you do it. At least kidneys are not unpleasant and slippery to handle, like liver and sweetbreads.

Procure

> 4 veal kidneys

Prepare them by removing white tissue and putting in a bowl containing

> 3 tablespoons vinegar

Toss as you add kidneys so all will be coated with vinegar. When they are fixed, cook till crisp, in a large pot

> 3 slices bacon

When fried, remove bacon. Brown the kidneys for about five minutes over medium heat in the fat, stirring often. Remove the browned cubes and set aside.

Now brown in the bacon fat, adding a little oil if necessary,

> 2 onions, sliced
>
> 1 clove garlic, split

Cook till the onions brown and lose their shape a little. Then add

> 4 cups stewed tomatoes
>
> ¼-1 cup red wine
>
> 1 cup vegetable stock or water
>
> 1½ teaspoon sweet basil
>
> 1 bay leaf
>
> ¼ teaspoon rosemary
>
> ¼ teaspoon oregano
>
> 1 tablespoon parsley
>
> 1 teaspoon salt, ¼ teaspoon black pepper
>
> 1 teaspoon sugar or honey

Rub all the herbs between your fingers before adding them. This is a very important thing and you should do it whenever you use herbs—it crushes the leaves and brings out the aromatic oils that give them their particular flavor. Cook the tomatoes and stuff together for about fifteen minutes.

Then add

> 2 stalks celery, with leaves, diced
>
> 2 carrots, diced
>
> 1 cup fresh peas
>
> 1½ cup fresh mushrooms, quartered
>
> 1 cup fresh corn, cut from the cob

and simmer tightly covered another fifteen minutes, or until vegetables are tender. Add the reserved kidneys, the reserved cooked crumbled bacon, and heat through. Serve immediately, without further heating, and with plenty of good bread to soak up the savory gravy.

SMOTHERED KIDNEY BEEF BURGERS

Remove all the white tissue, with scissors, from
 1 beef kidney
Grind it and mix it with
 ½ to ¾ pound lean ground beef
Season with
 1 tablespoon vinegar
 Salt, pepper
 Worcestershire sauce
 ½ onion finely chopped
Form into thin patties and using a little oil, brown *very quickly,* only enough to change color.
Remove kidneys from skillet and add to pan
 ½ onion, sliced
 2 stalks celery, sliced
Sauté quickly and add
 Canned tomatoes and juice to equal two cups
 ½ cup red wine
 Leaves from the celery, chopped fine
 1 teaspoon celery seed, crushed
 1 bay leaf
Simmer ten minutes, return the ground kidney patties to pan and heat through, about two minutes only, and serve immediately, with mashed potatoes or brown rice or biscuits or something to sop up the gravy. I like it this way, that is, thin. Some care for the gravy a little thicker, in which case a tablespoon of tomato paste or two should be added.

fowl

About a week before this writing, I read in *The New York Times* (so it must be true) that the government is going to allow cancerous chickens on the market, taking them off only when they are not, "æsthetically pleasing," i.e. having visible tumors, in which case they will be sold to the hot dog industry. This has convinced me more strongly than ever that one should eat only organic chickens. (That word again!) Although more expensive, much more than regular chickens (organic, 71¢ per pound; regular 29¢ to 40¢ per pound), still they are cheaper than other organic meat. Delicious, too, much better flavored, and less fatty.

This first is a recipe from Crispin's mother. It is really *good,* and has enough dressing for everybody, as it is not dressing that is in the chicken but . . .

CHICKEN IN DRESSING

Actually, I always called it stuffing. But west of some mysterious point in the middle of the U.S. it turns into dressing, and who can say why? Whenever anything here is stuffed, Ronnie goes through a thing with Michael and me with Crispin about which it is. Can I have more stuffing? You mean dressing? Also, about once a day, Crispin and I go through a thing about "bring" and "take." Can you bring this upstairs? Why yes, I imagine if I go up I could take it. Enough of such foolishness. Here is the recipe, as Crispin's mother sent it to me:

"Crescent, I don't have a recipe for this. I just put in the stuff and it usually comes out pretty good. I buy a good fat hen or a large fat fryer, but I prefer the hen because of the fat. Wash and cut up, or she could be left whole. I cook mine in a pressure cooker, but it could be stewed till tender. Do not overcook. Have lots of broth for the dressing. Bake a pan of corn bread and break it into a large mixing bowl, add

> 1 large chopped onion.
> Sage, sausage seasoning, and salt to taste (it takes
> very little salt because I salt chicken when I stew it)

I usually add black pepper, a little celery seed (some people add fresh chopped celery but my family doesn't like it). Add

> 4-6 hard-boiled eggs, chopped
> The chicken broth (it should be yellow with fat)

Stir and taste and stir and add a little more of this or that. When it tastes right to you, it is ready to bake. It should be a thin mixture.

Pour into a baking pan or dish or whatever you have. Push the chicken down into this mixture, a piece at a time, or if you leave the chicken whole, push it down into the center of the pan of dressing. Bake in a slow, 300°F. or less, oven for one hour or more. The longer the better. Sometimes you will need to add water to the dressing mixture to make it thin enough. It needs to be thin because it will dry out a lot when it is baking. I usually don't make gravy, but, if you like it, save some of your broth, a hard-boiled egg or two, the liver and the gizzard. Chop them into the broth. Mix a little flour in cold water and add to the broth. This is called giblet gravy.

I know this sounds silly, but that's the way I am. I really believe my main secret is that the dressing is really moist and the sausage seasoning. However it is good without the sausage seasoning and it might be difficult for you to find this. Ask at a meat market."

In a completely different but equally good vein is the delectable, slightly sour Puerto Rican Pickled Chicken, the recipe for which was given us by Merina Berkowitz. Merina is a case worker, she works with Big Diane, and she wanted to move in, and *we* wanted her to move in, but her landlord, naturally, wouldn't let her out of the lease. She stayed with us anyhow, about two weeks around Christmas. During that time she fixed this.

MERINA'S PICKLED CHICKEN

Rub a
> 3 pound chicken, cut in pieces

With
> Several cut cloves of garlic and an onion (rub well all over, getting into cracks and creases)

Brown the pieces in
> Oil in a skillet

When all the pieces are browned, place them in a large pot. Measure the oil left from browning and add enough to make ¾ cup. Add also
> 1 cup vinegar and
> Plenty of salt and pepper

Simmer, covered, 45 minutes, turning twice. This is even better when reheated, or if allowed to stand awhile.

Noble Chicken Curry is far removed from either chicken in dressing or pickled chicken; it is one of my all-time favorites.

Sooner or later you will have to learn how to make a cream sauce and it might as well be now. You need it in this recipe.

CREAM SAUCE

Melt over low heat
    2 tablespoons butter
Stir in
    2 tablespoons whole wheat flour
Gradually add, stirring constantly
    1 cup milk
Keep stirring until it thickens, a matter of a few minutes. You must have faith, and there you have it! Cream Sauce! This particular recipe is for a sauce of medium thickness—more butter and flour, always equal amounts, will make it thicken; less with make it thinner.

This is the basis for many many things. Add sugar and use half vinegar, half water for a sweet and sour sauce. Flake tuna, or cooked chicken, or lobster into it, add peas and pimento for color and then seasoning, salt and pepper, and maybe a touch of white wine or sherry if you want to be classy. Serve over toast, or rice or cornbread (this last is especially delicious) and you have tuna, chicken or lobster à la king! For Creamed Chipped Beef, soak dried beef in hot water for a few minutes, drain, dry and stir into the (your!) cream sauce. Season it. This too is delicious on cornbread. There is no reason not to serve it because you had it disgustingly dished out to you at school or in the army (where it is infamously known as "shit on shingles"). *This* bears no resemblance to the institutional breed. Anyway . . .

NOBLE CHICKEN CURRY

Stew as you would for chicken broth (page 33)
    1 frying chicken
Sauté some onions with a few more cloves than usual and add, if you like
    A slice of fresh ginger to the stewing water.

Simmer, uncovered, skimming occasionally, till the meat is tender, about an hour or less, if it's a young chicken. Fish the chicken pieces out of the broth, let cool, and pick the meat from the bones (no effort at all, at this point). *Save the stock.* Put the chicken, boned, aside. Discard the bones. Strain and measure the broth. Prepare as for cream sauce

> ¼ cup butter ⎫
> ¼ cup flour ⎬ per quart stock

Gradually add the stock, as you would the milk. (This sort of cream sauce, made with stock instead of milk, is technically known as a velouté sauce.) Cook till thickened. Though it may seem foolish, add back what you strained out and

> Curry powder to taste (mine is a *lot*!)

Now you may add any or all of the following things

> Raisins
> Pimentos
> Peas
> Parsley
> Crystallized ginger
> Grated lemon rind

And of course, add the chicken pieces.

Stir till heated through. Officially, it is done now, but if you want to be especially classy, just before serving add

> 1 cup coconut milk (see below)
> 1 tablespoon lime juice

And there you are! A chicken curry you can serve your most illustrious guests. It is ready to be served at once. Or it can wait without harm, for a bit.

Serve it with rice—plain or with a touch of saffron added during cooking. Also serve various sambals. A sambal, in case you didn't know, is a little dish of something to sprinkle on a curry. Grated coconut is almost necessary as is chutney, which you can make or buy. You can also make cranberry chutney or prune pickle. Simpler to do are finely chopped hard-boiled eggs; grated fresh apples; fresh bananas, sliced finely; raisins, if you didn't add them directly to the curry; and chopped nuts. Before I forget . . .

COCONUT MILK

Mix
> 1 cup fresh coconut, grated
> 1 tablespoon honey
> > *or*
> 1 can coconut (unhealthy)

With
> 1 cup scalded hot milk

Cover and let stand fifteen minutes. Squeeze every drop of milk from the coconut. It's flavorless now anyway. And that is coconut milk.

A typical Sunday night meeting. We will all be sitting around saying things like, "How much would you say a can of pineapple chunks costs?" Ronnie and Michael will have to go somewhere on Ronnie's night to cook and for some reason nobody can change nights with her. "Hmmm," Ronnie says, "Hmmm, Hmmm." "Why don't you make chicken baked in sour cream?" says Michael. "That's what I'll make," says Ronnie. "Chicken Baked in Sour Cream."

RONNIE'S CHICKEN BAKED IN SOUR CREAM

Combine equal parts of
> Cornmeal and whole wheat flour (for breading the chicken)

Season with
> Salt
> Onion salt
> Garlic salt
> Oregano, sage, thyme and caraway seeds

In the above mixture, bread
> 1 frying chicken

Set the pieces aside.

In a large skillet, heat

Oil and/or sweet butter

Sauté in it

1 or 2 onions, sliced

When tender and transparent, remove them and place them in a casserole.

Next, sauté in oil

½ pound mushrooms, sliced (or less—Ronnie likes mushrooms)

When tender, put them in the casserole. Now, sauté the chicken pieces till golden brown. Put them in the casserole. Heat in the skillet

1 pint water, milk, or chicken broth

Scrape the bottom to get flavorful bits stuck thereon. When hot, mix with it

1 pint sour cream

Pour this mixture over the chicken, onions, and mushrooms. Bake, covered, at 350°F. for about 50 minutes.

Uncover and add, if you like

⅓ cup white wine or cream sherry

Bake another ten minutes and serve with rice.

Though it is difficult to explain, there is a certain balance in Mike and Ronnie's conversation.

SCENE: *Michael and Ronnie come into the kitchen late at night. They've been out somewhere and seem very tired. The cat is on the floor playing with a dead fly. I sit snacking. They take some leftovers out of the refrigerator and eat. Michael is looking at a sculpture catalog rather listlessly. Ronnie is just eating staring straight ahead at the floor. Five or so minutes pass.*

MICHAEL: That cat has been playing with that fly since we came in.

(*They go on eating. Michael notices something he likes in the sculpture catalog.*)

MICHAEL: Hey, look at these warriors!

RONNIE: (*looking up*) Worriers?

MICHAEL: Warriors. (*He shows her the catalog.*)

RONNIE: Oh. I thought you said worriers.

(*They go back to eating and this continues for maybe another five minutes.*)

MICHAEL: (*suddenly*) Cat, can't you see that fly isn't gonna play with you no more? He's *Dead*.

RONNIE: (*Inexpressibly sad*) Oh. Dead?

Actually, what I am talking about, I guess, is the cross purpose conversation which takes someone else to see as funny.

SCENE: *The Dianes and I are sitting around the kitchen, again late at night, stoned, one summer evening, discussing the high incidence of strange bugs in the kitchen late at night.*

BIG DIANE: It's funny—there aren't many in my room. Are there in yours, Crescent?

(*I give this careful thought, and recall that yesterday, when I cleaned up, the floor under the big window fan was littered with dead bugs.*)

ME: Well, most of them get killed coming in through the fan.

To skip with alarming haste to another subject, here is another recipe of the chicken–cream school, from Jerry Rhea who was originally a friend of Diane Amorals, but now a friend to all of us. He is an incredible cook.

JERRY RHEA'S CHICKEN IN CREAM SAUCE

This is rather expensive and quite rich—almost decadent—but delicious.

Soak

    1 large frying chicken, cut in pieces

for about 2 hours in salted water (with a clove of garlic if you like).

While the chicken soaks, create the sauce.

Boil, in a small, heavy saucepan

> 4 cups chicken broth
>
> Salt, pepper, parsley, celery tops and marjoram
>
> ¼ teaspoon each—thyme and allspice

Boil 5 minutes, then simmer over low heat for about ½ hour, to reduce the stock to about half of its original volume. Strain. Dissolve

> 2 scant tablespoons whole wheat flour

in a little of the broth, strain this and add it to the rest of the broth. Stir over a low heat, until thick and smooth. Set aside. Now, slice

> ½ pound mushrooms
>
> 2 medium onions

Sauté these in

> 2 tablespoons butter

Add to the thickened stock with

> 1 cup heavy cream

Cook over low heat, stirring constantly, ten minutes. Remove from heat, stir in

> 4 ounces white wine

and set aside covered. Now, take the soaked chicken pieces, pat them dry with a paper towel and bread them in whole wheat flour seasoned with salt and pepper. Jerry Rhea does this by shaking the chicken pieces in a bag with the flour. Shake off excess flour and fry the chicken in a heavy skillet in

> ½ inch of oil (olive is nice)

When the chicken is browned on all sides, remove from the pan and drain. Pour out the oil, return the chicken to the pan and add

> 8 ounces more white wine

Cook over high heat till all the wine is boiled away. Place the chicken in a casserole, pour the sauce over it, cover and bake at 350°F. for 45 minutes.

This is the very last chicken recipe in here, and fittingly enough, it is one for leftover chicken, my own invention.

CHICKEN ROMANO WITH WATERCRESS

Dice
>Cooked leftover chicken
>
>1 small onion
>
>A few mushrooms (optional)

Brown these in a little butter and olive oil.
Sprinkle with
>Whole wheat flour

and stir well. Blend in
>a few tablespoons sour cream
>
>2 tablespoons cream sherry (the two will curdle but ignore it)
>
>Dash Tabasco, sage, ground coriander, salt
>
>Lots and lots of paprika
>
>A few generous handfuls fresh grated Parmesan–romano cheese combination

Only fresh grated will do. Cook, stirring often, till heated through. Just before serving, stir in
>A handful of chopped watercress

Serve immediately, rolled up in thin pancakes, if you like.

BASIC STUFFING

A good stuffing is the work of a fertile mind. Actually, the only thing people agree on that makes a good stuffing is moistness. Other than that, there is no consensus. Some people like a stuffing bland, some opulently flavored, some with lots of vegetables, some predominantly bread, some sweet, some not so sweet. Personally, I like stuffing with a lot of dried fruit chopped up in it. But here is a basic recipe, which you can vary as you see fit.

First, if it is stuffing for a chicken or turkey, cover giblets with water and cook over low heat till tender. Giblets are the heart, liver, and gizzard. Chop finely and reserve both giblets and broth. Now, mix the giblets with

3 cups or so whole-grain bread crumbs
1 or 2 chopped onions
1 or 2 chopped stalks of celery
Sage, parsley, marjoram, thyme, salt and pepper to
    taste
1 or 2 chopped hard-boiled eggs
½ can water chestnuts, chopped
1 raw egg and enough giblet broth to moisten a little

The above is a rather conservative sage dressing and one
that I wouldn't use without adding some or all of the following

½ cup each chopped dried apricots and/or prunes
½-1 cup chopped very tart firm cooking apples, with
    skins
Chopped nuts and raisins and orange sections
Orange juice to moisten
Corn bread crumbs instead of bread crumbs
Kasha, cooked, instead of bread crumbs
Brown rice, cooked and browned with onion instead
    of bread crumbs
Chopped blanched chestnuts and mushrooms

or any combination of the above. My favorites, really, are
stuffings with a base of corn bread or kasha, with dried apricots, apples, and prunes, a generous amount of chopped onion,
celery, hard-boiled egg and nuts.

There are two methods of roasting a chicken, one which
is useful when in a hurry, the other more leisurely. Actually,
the first is not technically roasting at all, as roasting is cooking
by dry heat and this method is steaming. The chicken is stuffed,
not too tightly, as the dressing will expand, and sewed or laced
up (that is, small skewers, nails or toothpicks are crisscrossed
to close it, and then laced like a boot). Paprika is rubbed all
over it, to give it a golden color, and it is rubbed with a cut
lemon. It is then covered tightly and baked at 350°F. about
forty-five minutes to an hour.

The other method is to oil the chicken all over, place it on
a rack above a pan in the oven and bake at 250°F. for about
an hour per pound, or at 300°F. about 45 minutes per pound.
Both methods are good. (Cooking times are for stuffed bird.)

fish and seafood

As of this writing, Ronnie is a vegetarian. Actually, she just doesn't eat meat. She *does* eat milk and eggs and cheese and fish and seafood, which I guess, doesn't make her a true vegetarian. At any rate, she and Michael cook most of the fish and shellfish that gets eaten around here. Their favorite is shrimp, and quite often they fix it, usually mixed with vegetables and soy sauce and nuts, sometimes sweet-sour, sometimes not. Often they also fix fish fillets (3 pounds fish fillets—whatever's cheap, they write on their menus) which are usually just broiled quickly with plenty of butter and soy sauce and perhaps a few sliced mushrooms and onions. The recipes that follow, then, are for the most part theirs.

MICHAEL AND RONNIE'S SHRIMP AND PSEUDO-SHRIMP DISH, SWEET-SOUR

The pseudo shrimp are the cashews. Wait and see.
In
     2 tablespoons oil
Brown
     1 pound shrimp

    1 green pepper, seeded and sliced

    1 carrot, sliced

    1½-2 cups fresh pineapple (or canned unsweetened) cut in chunks

    1 cup cashews, raw or otherwise

Meanwhile, make the sauce (the secret, Michael told me, with a glint in his eye).

Combine

    ¼ cup wine, cream sherry, preferably

    ½ cup soy sauce

    ½ cup unsweetened pineapple juice

    1 tablespoon molasses

    1 tablespoon honey

Stir well. Heat through and serve over shrimp mixture with plenty of brown rice.

SUMMER SHRIMPS

Mix together

    1½ cups apple cider vinegar

    1 cup oil

    ¼-½ cup honey

    ½ clove of garlic, pressed

    1 tablespoon grated onion

    ½ teaspoon salt

    ¼ teaspoon ginger

    Dash each mace and ground cloves

    1 large green pepper, seeded and finely chopped

Marinate in the above for several hours

    3 cups fresh shrimp, shelled and deveined, and cooked slightly

When ready to serve, stir in

    2 cups fresh pineapple chunks

    2 large tomatoes, chopped

    1 large ripe avocado, chopped (save the pit to start a plant)

Serve on lettuce—a good supper for a hot summer night.

SEVICHE CON ALCAPARRAS
(A Mexican marinated raw fish appetizer from Jo An)

Bone, skin and cut into tiny pieces
> 1 pound fresh white fish

Marinate and chill the fish for several hours in a porcelain bowl in
> ¾ cup lemon juice
> 1 teaspoon salt
> ¼ teaspoon freshly ground pepper

Add and chill further
> 3 canned seeded chili peppers (jalapeño) finely chopped
> 2 medium-sized tomatoes, peeled and cut up
> 1 large onion chopped or grated finely
> 2 tablespoons capers
> 4 tablespoons olive oil
> 2 tablespoons dry white wine or vinegar
> 2 teaspoons oregano

Serve very cold in chilled cocktail glasses or shells garnished with sliced avocado and parsley sprigs.

vegetable entrees

A lot of people we know are vegetarians, with their own reasons for eating thus and their own definitions of a good vegetarian's eating habits. Their reasons range from moral and physical to political to I-like-the-way-it-tastes-better and I-get-high-easier reasons. Their habits cover the range of no meat but fish okay, no fish but dairy products okay, no dairy products, but only vegetables, and any combination of the above.

I really don't mean to sound cynical. I've had enough vegetarian meals to know how good they can be (Ronnie and Little Diane are kind of halfway vegetarians) and enough long raps with vegetarians to know how good *they* can be. I, however, don't believe that eating healthy animals is immoral or unhealthy. There should be no alienation of human being from animal. For persons who eat animals but cannot imagine eating other people generally assume that animals have no souls, that they are nothing but flesh or meat and that humans solely possess a soul, and neither is true. I honestly can see a certain sort of "liberated meat eating" involving persons who eat the whole animal and who do that because they love it, because they want to incorporate its flesh and essence with theirs.

Most vegetarians I know are city people, they have never had contact with animals raised as food; they have no understanding of eating as loving and no contact with nature. I don't know any country people who are vegetarians (I don't *think*). Country people see the "violence" in nature, they see clearly the deer needs the wolf, for instance, though one may kill the other. In closer terms, they scratch behind the ears of what will some day be supper and love it deeply, alive *and* on the table. Crispin, for instance, is a country person. He grew up on a farm in western Texas, and he is gentle and beautiful and wonderful to see with animals and everything else. Our cat had a wounded tail, swollen and puffed up and full of pus, so painful she held it in an odd way. How it happened I don't know— but Crispin sterilized a knife and lanced it. It was a hard job, at least it would have been hard for me, but he did it, easily, loving the cat, helping it heal. Crispin loves animals so strongly. And he eats meat. It is not that there is a conflict that he hasn't seen—he has thought about it and he knows how intricately bound life and death, love and hate, violence and gentleness are, so closely that they are the same thing, so closely that I have to restrain myself from putting quotation marks about all those words.

But . . . some people are vegetarians. While I, as you can see, disagree strongly, I believe in their right—of course!—to be vegetarians, or whatever else they want to be, and eat what they believe is best for them, and it may indeed be. And, as I said earlier, I have learned that a meatless meal can be delicious. So, here are some recipes from vegetarian or semi-vegetarian friends for entrees. Before I give them to you, a warning, though, to all would-be and already-are vegetarians. Get a good knowledge of nutrition first off. It is certainly possible, though difficult, to fulfill all basic nutritional needs with vegetables and perhaps a few supplements, but you have to know *which* gives the required grams of protein a day. Much of this can be supplied for vegetarians from soybeans and wheat germ, both high-quality vegetable protein sources. But you need to know. These are just examples. So please, read up on it, in several different books, before you start. Read Ohsawa *and* Adelle Davis *and* Carlton Fredericks *and* everybody, so you can get some idea of what the general opinion is and then decide what *your* ideal diet is. Now, then—the recipes.

SOY RECIPES

Soybeans, as I mentioned earlier, are extraordinary sources of protein, as well as other nutrients. A cup of them, cooked plain, for instance, supplies 22 grams of protein, 5.4 of iron, 150 mg calcium, 360 mg phosphorus, 1,080 mg potassium, 1,180 international units Vitamin A, .1 mg Vitamin B, .2 mg Vitamin B2, 1.3 mg niacin. They are some 18-22 percent oil, and soy oil is one of the richest known sources of lecithin. Lecithin is a fat-soluble substance which breaks up and helps the body utilize fats and fatty substances. At any rate, soybeans are very good for you. They don't taste bad either, just very very bland, a bit chicken-like. They respond well if they are treated with a good spicy or well-seasoned cream sauce. And they can be added to many things—soups, stews—to enrich them. Ground, or in flour or powdered form, they enrich even more things— french toast, casseroles, ground meat. But these last, obviously, are not vegetarian, and it seems to me that one of the primary functions of soybeans is to fulfill the needs of someone who, for one reason or another, has eliminated meat as a source of protein. So, here goes.

BASIC SOYBEAN PREPARATION

The basic method of cooking soybeans starts the night before you want them.

Soybeans
are placed in
Water to cover

with perhaps a slice of onion added for flavor. In the morning they are cooked in their soaking water until tender, about three hours. They are now ready to be eaten as a side dish with nought save butter and salt, or sauced or loafed or pattied or balled up in any of the following ways.

MIKE AND RONNIE'S SOYBEAN DELIGHT

Cook, as directed,
>2 cups uncooked soybeans

After they are tender, keep them warm while you make the following sauce.

Brown
>3 onions
>1 pound mushrooms

In
>a lot of butter

Set this aside and stir into the butter they were browned in, plus a little more perhaps
>3 tablespoons buckwheat flour

Stir till quite smooth, and then gradually add, while stirring
>2 cups milk

Add the browned mushrooms and onions and cook them in the cream sauce (or white sauce, technically, as no cream was used herein) about five minutes. Add the soybeans and cook another five minutes.

This sounds innocuous but it is really good.

SOYBEAN SOUP-STEW

Soak overnight and cook until tender
>1 cup dry soybeans

When tender, add
>½ head cabbage, sliced thickly
>3 cloves garlic
>1 bay leaf
>3 whole peppercorns
>3 whole allspice
>Pinch each basil, oregano, thyme
>3 ears of corn, each cut in thirds, with the kernels left on the cob

       2 onions, quartered
       1-2 potatoes, sliced
       1 cup shelled peas, preferable fresh
       1 cup or more raw string beans
       4 cups tomatoes
       Lots of salt and pepper

Cover and cook about ten to fifteen minutes. Serve in bowls, with cheese on crackers.

SWEET-SOUR SOYBALLS

Grind in a meat grinder
       3 cups cooked soybeans (1 heaping cup dry)
Mix with them
       ¼ cup dried parsley
       ½ teaspoon each salt and kelp
Form into balls, the size depending on whether this is to be main dish or appetizer. Make a batter by beating together
       1 beaten egg
       1 tablespoon water
       2 tablespoons whole wheat flour
       ¼-½ teaspoons ground pepper
Roll the soyballs around in it. Heat in a skillet
       ¼-½ cup oil
Roll the battered soyballs around in the hot oil until well browned. Remove from skillet and drain all but 1 tablespoon of oil.
       Add to that
       2 green peppers, cut in wedges
       5 pineapple rings, cut in pieces
       1 carrot, cut in strips
       ½ cup stock (vegetable cooking water or from broth powder)
Cover and cook over medium heat 10 minutes. Meanwhile blend
       3 tablespoons cornstarch

1 tablespoon soy sauce
½ cup unsweetened pineapple juice
½ cup vinegar (cider)
¼ cup honey

Add to vegetables and stir till thickened. Return soyballs to pan, stir 3 minutes and serve.

Here are some non-soybean-based vegetarian entrees.

SEED-STUFFED PEPPERS

This is a dish Crispin had with a vegetarian in Colorado. They're very good and quite rich—few people will be able to eat more than one.

Cut off the tops, scoop out the insides and any bad parts of
6 large green peppers

If you have a vegetable steamer, cut them in half lengthwise and steam for about ten minutes. This can also be done by putting them on a rack above boiling water and covering tightly. If neither are available, they may be dropped into boiling water to blanch; however this last process destroys the Vitamin C and flavor. At any rate, after they have been treated in any one of these ways, stuff them with a filling made by grinding
1 pound sunflower seeds
½ pound pumpkin seeds

Add
4 carrots, grated
1 large or two small onions, grated or chopped
4 stalks celery, sliced

Mix all together in a large bowl and season with
Salt, pepper, thyme
Onion salt, garlic salt,
Parsley, basil, rosemary

After each pepper is stuffed, put it into a greased casserole which has a little
>Tomato juice

poured into the bottom. Bake at 350°F. until heated through, about fifteen minutes.

EGGPLANT PARMIGIANA

This is very nearly my favorite vegetarian dish. It is one Ronnie makes frequently.

First mix up an uncooked sauce of
>1 can tomatoes
>1 can tomato puree
>Rosemary, oregano, basil, thyme, parsley (all to taste)

Now, slice an eggplant lengthwise and dip in a mixture of
>Whole wheat flour
>Cornmeal

Fry in oil till golden brown. Layer the fried eggplant and sauce with
>1 pound mozzarella cheese
>½ cup soy grits

Top with sauce and sprinkle well with
>Parmesan cheese
>Wheat germ.

Bake at 350°F. till bubbling hot. Serves about 4.

vegetables as side dishes

Now we come to vegetables as what most people consider their rightful place: side dishes. Many vegetables are often perfect with nothing more than a little butter and salt added, if cooked correctly, that is, until still crisp, flavorful, and vitamin-rich. But vegetables are also good, depending on which one, when cooked with a little cheese or sour cream or another vegetable, or a few spices and/or herbs, knowingly selected. Rather than give you directions for specifically cooking each different kind of vegetable, I'll give you a few general hints. I'll also lay on you some of my favorite special ways to cook certain vegetables.

In general then: water is the villain. As little water as possible should touch vegetables in order to preserve the utmost flavor and nutritional value. When you wash vegetables, dry them immediately thereafter. And *don't* soak them! This useless pastime takes nothing but time and energy and vitamins. And never add vitamin-destroying soda to "keep the color." Also, in most cases, avoid peeling them. The peel is often the best-tasting part, and most of the vitamins and minerals lurk therein. In things like mashed potatoes, mash the peel right in. It won't look *too* funny, it will taste better, and save you a lot of work. Peel things *only* when the skin is bitter, very tough or heavily sprayed. All right. Back to water. Don't drop your nice, un-

101

peeled vegetables into boiling water. If at all possible, steam them either in a pot with a rack therein and a tight-fitting lid or, watching closely, with a very small bit of water in which the vegetables cook directly and, again, a tight-fitting lid. They will burn, though, if you're not careful.

SPINACH WITH SOUR CREAM

Spinach shrinks to almost nothing as if by magic. A pound will feed only three people. In this recipe, it is cooked only enough to get hot, but should not wilt.

Per pound of spinach, slice
> About 4 or 5 mushrooms

Brown them well in
> A little butter

With
> A clove of garlic

When the mushrooms have shrunk slightly and are quite brown, remove them from the heat. Take the garlic out and contribute it to the soup bag or chew it as you continue (it's not too strong at this point, the flavor having dissolved into the butter). Now mix the mushrooms with

> 1 pound or a bit less spinach, *thoroughly* washed, thoroughly dried and chopped

If spinach is not washed it will be sandy. And if it is not dried well after being washed, you will experience this weird, unpleasant sort of coated-rubbing-wrong-way-feeling on your teeth, which has something to do with the oxalic and phytic acids dissolving out. At any rate (if I have not scared you out of it) toss the spinach leaves with

> ¼ cup sour cream, or more—up to a cup
> ¼-½ cup freshly grated Parmesan cheese

Put the treated spinach into a greased casserole and bake at 350°F. about 10-15 minutes, until heated through but still crispish.

JAPANESE SPINACH

This should be served quite cold, so prepare it a few hours before serving and let it chill in the refrigerator.

Cook

     Frozen spinach, as much as is needed

Chill deeply. Dress with

     Soy sauce

     Oil

     Sesame seeds

Serve cold.

STRING BEANS WITH TOMATOES

String beans have an affinity for tomatoes, which, in turn, have an affinity for basil, so this dish works out very nicely.

Put

     A very little bit of water

in a pot that has a lid (or something) that fits it securely. Drop into it

     1 pound string beans, with ends cut off and thrown in the soup bag

Cover and let cook while you quarter

     Several tomatoes, 2, 3 or 4

Add them and

     About half a teaspoon basil, crushed between the fingers.

Continue cooking till the string beans are tenderish, about ten to fifteen minutes altogether. This is a good recipe as is or with a few slices of onion added during cooking. Or drained and tossed with grated cheddar cheese. Or served chilled, or chilled and mixed with bean sprouts. Or with a dribble of butter added.

GENIE'S HARVARD-STYLE BEETS

Personally, I don't like beets. But Genie Reese does, although they look terrible on the flaming orange plates that she and Ray have. This is her recipe for them, Harvard Style (sweet-sour).

Mix together

    1 tablespoon cornstarch

    2 tablespoons flour

    ½ cup raw sugar (or less)

    A dash ground cloves (optional)

Carefully stir in, averting lumps (I mean, beets are bad enough)

    ¼ cup each vinegar and water

Drain, reserving juice

    1 can beets

Mix the flour-vinegar mixture into the beet juice over a low flame, beating, beating, all the while. A wire whisk makes this easier.

When smooth and thickened, just before serving time, add the beets and

    3 tablespoons butter

Toss and serve.

MIDDLE EASTERN EGGPLANT

Simmer together over low heat about fifteen minutes

    1 can tomatoes in juice

    ½ eggplant, chopped, with peel

    1 tablespoon dried mint

Actually, this isn't really authentically Middle Eastern, but it tastes like it.

Another sweet-sour dish I enjoy is

SWEET-SOUR CABBAGE

Brown
    1 onion, chopped
In
    Oil, fat, butter, or bacon fat (this last is preferable
        tastewise, but not DDT-wise)
till golden. Add
    4 cups shredded cabbage, red or green or a com-
        bination
    3-5 tart apples, diced, cored but not peeled
    1 tablespoon apple-cider vinegar
    ½ cup water or apple cider
    3 teaspoons caraway seeds
    ½ cup raisins
    Salt to taste
    Dash each cinnamon and allspice
Cover and cook slowly till tender. Before serving you may
add (I don't) some red wine.

The next recipe is from Mrs. Miller, our landlady, who
only recently battled with the sanitation men to remove some
stuff that the fire department had declared a hazard. (That was
weird—we had a little fire in the basement one day, something
caught from our furnace. Michael called the Fire Department.
It was out when they arrived, but they came anyway—rain-
coated and belted and poled and speared and roped and looking thoroughly silly, especially that early in the morning. Ronnie took some pictures of them till they told her to stop. Later
the captain (or whoever) was taking down the details, and our
conversation went like this:
HIM: Mr. James Miller, right?
ME: *Reverend* James Miller
HIM: (*worriedly*) Oh, gee, I put down mister here, do you
think that's all right?

I magnanimously assured him that it probably is. Anyway, it was funny, but they ordered us to clean out our basement in twenty-four hours (it really was kind of a mess—the house had lots of old furniture in it when we moved in and what we couldn't use we just threw on down). So then the Sanitation Department wouldn't come and pick up what we cleaned out, etc., etc., etc., as anyone who has lived in New York for awhile knows, and the whole thing was a lot like *Alice's Restaurant*, as any encounter with the bureaucracy is. Anyway, Mrs. Miller's carrots:

BAKED GLAZED MINTED CARROTS

Slice and put in a greased casserole
    1 bunch of carrots
Drizzle over them
    1½ teaspoons salt
    ¼ cup fresh chopped mint
    Honey
Dot with
    3 tablespoons butter
Bake at 350°F. for about an hour and cover. If you don't care about being healthy, substitute ¼ cup brown sugar for the honey.

Mint, incidentally, grows almost anywhere and like wildfire. In the little garden behind our house we planted tomatoes, radishes, beans and carrots. The radishes and beans did well and then fell into a decline that proved fatal (I got that phrase from Edward Gorey). On closer examination, it was apparent that this was due to aphids, tiny green bugs. The tomatoes were really doing well for awhile to the point where we could go out and pick a whole handful of little ripe cherry tomatoes. But one morning we went out and there were no more leaves, let alone tomatoes, on those poor plants. Overnight . . . gone. Crispin said some tomato worms had gotten them, which sounded likely to me. The carrots never showed up at all. We also had some pot growing there, three kinds, all excellent. The pot really flourished—I mean it did a whole lot better than anything else in the garden. When it was about four feet high we had some trouble with the cops. Not about *it*, mind you—a record player of ours was stolen and they caught the guy who did it, illegally. Like, we hadn't reported it or anything, we didn't know it was missing till someone knocked on the door and told us. On the way to the station house the guy asked us to 1) say that we had reported it missing three days ago, and 2) scratch a mark into it so when we got to the station house we wouldn't have trouble proving it was ours. Well, we wouldn't do either, and when we got there we wouldn't press charges and they were kind of pissed. In fact, they threatened to sub-poena us, and when that didn't work, they just withheld the record player and made it very hassle-y for us to get it. We finally did, about a week and many subway tokens-worth all around the city later. (That was before we knew about peo-ple's tokens—Jamaica half pennies—and slipping under the turnstiles.) Anyhow, we were afraid of further harassment (groundless, it has proven thus far, 3 or 4 months later), so we pulled it up. We dried it out in the oven and smoked it and honest to God, even though it wasn't supposed to be harvested that soon it was absolutely the best grass I have ever tasted. I guess it all cross-pollinated with each other and us. . . .

Anyhow, by midsummer, we were all getting rather dis-couraged with our garden. Then my mother gave us some pars-ley, sage, mint, and basil plants. We planted them right outside the kitchen door so they could easily be reached. The parsley promptly died. The sage grew till the cats discovered it. And then—it was absolutely amazing!—they smothered it. They would lie on it, roll on it, get high on it. The cats from next door came over to join the fun, and pretty soon there was no more sage. But the basil and mint spread and spread, and flour-ished, and flourished. And you use them in a lot of things. . . .

To our everlasting credit, however, and to those people

who say that hippies (not that that's what we are) never do
anything or finish anything, or that we're all like those people
in *Easy Rider* who appear to be planting dust in dry sand, we
really fixed up the garden itself. It was all old shoes, baby car-
riages, bottles, pipes, cement blocks. We completely cleared
the area, which was *really* a job. And then we fertilized it with
cow dung and peat moss. So maybe the next people that come
here can have a garden. Also, at that time we had no knowledge of organic gardening methods, something we have since
studied, and, also it must be a rare plant that can grow in New
York City air. Three (basil, mint, and pot) out of nine (tomatoes, radishes, carrots, beans, sage, parsley) is not so bad.

BAKED POTATOES

Baked potatoes are really good, a nice, humble vegetable
that I always forget about until I have it at my mother's and
then make the following week. This is how you do it.
    Scrub well
        Idaho or baking potatoes
Prick each of them a few times with a fork. (If you don't
they will explode! and your oven will look like the inside of a
cavern.) It will probably take at least an hour for them to bake,
at 375°F. The process can be speeded up a bit, though, by
sticking a clean nail into each potato. I suppose that conducts
the heat, or some such. These are excruciatingly delicious when
buttered, salted, sour creamed, and chived.

STUFFED POTATOES

Leftover baked potatoes may be stuffed.
    Split the potatoes lengthwise, scoop out most of the inside
and mash with
        Grated cheddar cheese
        A little evaporated and powdered milk
        Salt, cayenne pepper

Stuff and sprinkle with
Paprika
Dried parsley
Bake at 350°F. about fifteen minutes. They come out quite pretty to look at, golden brown and puffed slightly on top.

Any kind of leftover potato may be diced and fried with onions, plain or in bacon fat with some sort of leftover meat, and, in either case, is mighty passable instead of bread for breakfast.

POTATO PANCAKES

A friend of Big Diane's, Shelley, contributes this.
Grate, saving all juices
5 pounds large potatoes (leave skins on)
Add
¼ cup matzoh meal (or non-instant milk powder)
1 teaspoon salt
A little grated onion (optional but good)
Shape into little cakes and fry until brown in plenty of *hot* oil.

SWEET POTATOES

Sweet potatoes are also good. I should make them more often than I do: Christmas and Thanksgiving. The initial treatment of these applies to mashing white potatoes too.
Wash, *leave peel on,* and slice
Sweet potatoes
Put them into a pot in which a little water is boiling. Cover tightly and cook till tender, some twenty minutes. Now mash them vigorously, with peel. You see? You can't tell.

Now season with

    Molasses, cinnamon, raisins, ginger

    or brown sugar, cinnamon, raisins, ginger

    or honey, orange juice and rind, ginger

    or rum and vanilla

    or maple syrup and nutmeg and cinnamon

    or with pineapple cut into chunks and grated coconut

Whichever (and all are good), dot well with butter and brown under the broiler to reheat. This freezes well.

ACORN SQUASH

This vegetable is really pretty. Cut it in half (the little ones) and place them, cut-side up, in a baking pan with a little hot water in the bottom. Save the seeds: for beads, or to be dried slowly and used, shelled, like pumpkin or sunflower seeds, or for the soup bag. Sprinkle with any of the things used for sweet potatoes and dot with butter and in addition stick two cloves in either side of the squashes. Cover (a baking sheet on top is fine) and bake at 350°F. until tender, about half an hour or perhaps longer if the squash is big. A half will be too much for one person—people can share. And that about does it on the cooked vegetable score. So—we come to raw vegetables—salads.

salads

SUPER SALAD

There is only *one way* to make a salad which I have learned since the first writing of this book. It is little trouble and it is *so good* that you will never again make anything else or, at least, rarely. It is a very vigorously tossed salad—indeed, unless you have a very large salad bowl, count on losing some of it during the process. We use a cut-glass punch bowl that was here when we moved in. The bowl should be chilled if possible. This is often not possible as the refrigerator is often too crowded to accommodate it. After being chilled it is rubbed with a clove of garlic pounded with about a teaspoon of basil leaves. The garlic may be left in the bowl or added to the soup bag. Then, washed and *dried* salad greens are torn into it with the hands—lettuce, iceberg and romaine, chicory, endive, escarole, whatever. A variety is nice. About 2 tablespoons each chopped green onions and tops and finely chopped fresh parsley is added, all *dry*. Sliced carrots, little wedges of raw cauliflower or broccoli, or cheese or chicken or fish are added. Now, pour in a few tablespoons salad oil. The oil *must* be added previous to the vinegar or lemon juice, and a prepared dressing *must not* be used. Toss—that is, corner some of the greens between two spoons and hurl gently (is that a contradiction in terms?) a *lot*. The leaves *must* be completely coated with oil for this to taste extraordinary. They should glisten all over. Now, add juice of ¼ of a lemon, about a teaspoon salt (or less is you use kelp too), a dash Tabasco, kelp, and paprika. Serve *immediately,* garnished with anything so soft as to be untossable, like chopped hard-boiled eggs or avocados. I hold that nothing very moist, such as tomatoes, should be added to the salad but should be served along with it. I got most of these ideas from Adelle Davis, who calls salad making "The most important recipe in this book." No argument there.

Actually, these next aren't salad salads, but combinations of chilled fruits and vegetables. Most of these combinations are quite good.

FRUIT AND VEGETABLE
SALAD COMBINATIONS

Pineapple chunks,
   unsweetened
Bananas
Avocados
Cooked young peas

Cantaloupe
Orange sections
Carrots
Parsley
Lettuce

Cooked string beans
Lettuce
Raisins
Walnuts
Fennel seeds (ground)

Apples
Oranges
Bermuda onions
Green peppers
On lettuce with mint

Grapefruit sections
Orange sections
Pineapple chunks
Tomato wedges
Avocado

Tomatoes
Cucumbers
Scallions
Black olives
Radishes
On lettuce

Asparagus stalks, cooked
On lettuce, with onion rings
   on top
Mustard-mayonnaise
   dressing
Mushrooms, raw
With onion rings on lettuce
Sprinkled with lemon juice,
   salt, and black pepper

Broccoli, cooked and chilled
Tomato slices
Hard-boiled egg
Garlic salt
Tomato wedges
Sprinkled with fresh basil

And this is good, too, but very rich.

AVOCADO DELIGHT

Peel, pit, and cut in half
   One ripe avocado
Sprinkle it well with
   Lemon juice
Soften
   3 ounces cream cheese
Blend with
   2 tablespoons heavy cream or evaporated milk
   1 tablespoon lemon juice
   1 tablespoon finely chopped chives
   3 tablespoons almonds, chopped
   3 tablespoons ripe olives, chopped
   Salt, paprika and nutmeg to taste
Stuff the avocado halves with the above mixture. Press together firmly. Wrap in waxed paper, secure with toothpicks and chill very well—at least four hours. Serve on lettuce, with French dressing, sliced about half an inch thick.

BAKED TOMATO GARNISHES

Halve
   tomatoes (good ones, not the mealy, hothouse variety)

Sprinkle them with
> Bread crumbs
> Parsley
> Basil
> Parmesan cheese

Bake at 350°F. till tops are browned and tomatoes are heated through, about fifteen minutes. Serve as a garnish with steak (ha!).

JAPANESE PICKLED VEGETABLES

I *know* this is not really how you do it, but it's much quicker and simpler than the regular way and tastes quite authentic.

Layer in a nonmetal dish
> Thin slices of radishes
> Thin slices of cucumber, unpeeled, but the skin scored
> with a fork

Between layers sprinkle heavily with salt. Finish with a layer of salt on top. Add cold water not quite to cover and chill about half an hour. Drain, rinse under cold running water, and serve with some sort of Japanese dinner.

FRUIT SALADS

BASIC FRUIT SALAD

Combine any or all of the following
> Orange sections
> Grapefruit sections
> Tart apples, diced
> Bananas, sliced
> Pineapple chunks
> Strawberries, fresh
> Melon balls (cantaloupe and/or honeydew—I like
> these frozen with little icy centers)

Again, don't limit yourself. Add other seasonal fruits, some that most people won't recognize, like persimmon, Chinese gooseberry, and cactus fruits. Some fruits have a tendency to brown easily, which means they're losing Vitamin C. To avoid this, slice bananas and apples at the last possible minute and sprinkle with lemon juice. You might also want to try adding to your fruit salads

Anise

Fennel seeds

Fresh ginger root, a touch, grated

Cinnamon

Dash ground cloves

Raisins and other dried fruits (can be plumped up by putting in boiling water and letting the fruit sit therein for fifteen-thirty minutes. Reserve water for use in bread or in Fruit Soup.)

A bit of grated orange, lemon or lime rind

Mint leaves, fresh chopped or dry

I personally feel that fruit salad is best without dressing, but you may differ with me. If you do, you will find some at the end of the next chapter. I do, however, sometimes enjoy a large scoop of cottage cheese on it, for a pleasant and high-protein lunch, especially enjoyable in the summer.

LITTLE GREENIE
(a special fruit salad)

Mix together lightly

2 grapefruits, peeled and cut into sections

3 oranges, prepared the same as grapefruits

2 avocados, ripe, peeled, cut in chunks

½ a honeydew melon, cut from shell into chunks

½ pound seedless green grapes

1 cucumber, if desired, peeled, and cut into chunks

A few sprigs fresh mint, or 1 teaspoon dry mint, crushed between your fingers

DRESSING (especially for Little Greenie)
Combine in a blender and blend till smooth

½ cup mayonnaise

½ cup sour cream or plain yogurt

2 tablespoons lemon juice (omit if yogurt is used)

1 tablespoon mint, fresh (1½ teaspoon dry)

2 apricots or peaches—fresh if available, peeled, chopped and seeded, or 5 dried apricots, soaked in boiling water 15 minutes and chopped fine

Vigorous dash of salt

1 tablespoon honey

salad dressings

Mayonnaise is something that goes into a lot of things: sandwiches and eggs and salads and so forth. The kind you buy in the store does not have its ingredients on the label (legally it doesn't have to—they are "fixed" by the government) and I don't trust it. Whatever is in it—which preservatives and bleaches (the homemade kind comes out more yellow, so I wonder)—it is certainly not made with cold-pressed oil, as the kind at home can be. It's really easy to do, too.

HOMEMADE MAYONNAISE

Put into a blender
    2 egg yolks
    ½ teaspoon salt
    ½ teaspoon mustard
    ½ teaspoon honey
    1-2 teaspoons lemon juice or mild vinegar
Turn on blender and, while going, pour in very gradually
    1-2 cups oil
The more oil you use the thicker it will be. After oil has been added, stop and . . . you got it!

117

BASIC FRENCH DRESSING

Blend
> ½ cup cider or herb vinegar
> 3 teaspoons salt
> 2¼ teaspoons dry mustard
> 1 teaspoon freshly ground black pepper
> ½ teaspoon honey

Add
> 1 clove garlic

Let stand a few days, three or four, say, refrigerated. Shake every so often to blend flavor. Remove the garlic. Pour in
> 2 cups good salad oil

This makes a *lot* but that's okay because it improves on standing and is used frequently. It is very good as a marinade and can also be varied almost indefinitely. Remember, this *cannot* be used prepared on tossed salads. Oil and vinegar *must* be added separately.

VARIATIONS

Add any of the following to a night's worth of French Dressing.

Roquefort cheese (Blue)	Curry
Tabasco sauce	Tomato juice
Fine¹y chopped dill pickles	Rosemary
Capers	Sage
Onion juice	Parsley
Thyme	Cayenne pepper
Celery seed	Basil
Worcestershire sauce	Tarragon
Chili sauce	Caraway seed
Chopped hard-boiled egg	

RUSSIAN DRESSING

I really like this, for some reason, though it is very unhealthy, unless you have good mayonnaise and catsup on hand. That's all it is.

> 1 part catsup
> 5 parts mayonnaise

It is delightful on lettuce wedges with croutons.

HORSERADISH DRESSING

Blend

> 1½ cups sour cream or whipped cream
> 2 teaspoons horseradish, a little more, a little less, according to your taste

This simple dressing is a miracle on cold leftover meats as well as salads.

EASY GREEN GODDESS

Mix

> 1½ cups mayonnaise
> 1½ tablespoons of a combination of parsley, chives, sage, basil, tarragon, rosemary
> Pinch each dry mustard and garlic salt
> 1-2 teaspoons anchovy paste or finely chopped anchovies

FRUIT SALAD DRESSINGS

GINGER-CREAM DRESSING

Combine

> ½ cup heavy cream, whipped
> ½ cup mayonnaise
> 1 large slice fresh ginger root
> 1-3 tablespoons honey
> Dash salt

FRUIT FRENCH

Shake together
> ¼ cup orange juice
> 1 teaspoon lemon juice
> 2 tablespoons oil
> 1 tablespoon honey
> Salt to taste
> ½-¼ teaspoon dried mint leaves

CREAMY FRUIT FRENCH

Mix
> 2 tablespoons grapefruit juice, or 1 tablespoon each
> lemon and grapefruit juice
> ½ cup oil
> ½ cup honey
> ⅓ cup yogurt, sour cream, or heavy cream
> A few chopped nuts
> ½ teaspoon mint leaves
> Few drops rose water, if desired

See also Little Greenie Dressing, page 116.

grains

When people think of a healthy diet, often they think: brown rice. This is due to Georges Ohsawa, the father of Macrobiotics. Any one of his books can tell you much more than I could or even would. Suffice it to say, he feels that a balance between acid and alkaline, yin and yang, should be maintained at all times, 5 parts yin to 1 part yang, and that brown rice is the only food which has this balance, and all other foods must be balanced with each other. As the reader should be able to tell by now, I don't hold with this view *at all!* However, the house does eat a lot of brown rice. It is a cheap good staple and sops up gravies as well as anything. The husk, too, has a good quantity of the B Vitamins. It is not difficult to cook—it is all a question of knowing how.

There are other, more interesting grains to use as carbohydrates. One is kasha, or buckwheat groats, which has a rather distinctive nutty flavor and is good as stuffing (dressing). Whole wheat can be cooked, the grain, not the flour, and it's good too. And bulgar, and couscous, which are various kinds of wheat (I *think*—we never got this one quite straightened out —what the difference is and where they came from) are nice and cook quickly to boot. I prefer couscous to bulgar—the latter seeming too flaky for me (you'll see what I mean when you cook it). Millet is also relatively quick cooking and pleasant textured.

There are basically two methods of cooking all grains. In one, water or other liquid is brought to a vigorous boil and then rice or whatever is added slowly, stirred in and cooked till all the water is absorbed. In the other, butter or oil is heated, the grains are rolled around till well coated therein, and then a suitable amount of hot or boiling liquid is added. More liquid is necessary with the former method. If either of these rules is followed closely the grains will not be gummy—the water *boiling* prevents this. Very simple, but it works.

BASIC RICE

Now rice *must* be washed. I never knew it came dirty. I thought that peculiar brown ring that formed on the top was just something that routinely happened to rice, until Little Diane set me straight—it's *dirt*. The rice should be washed under *cold* running water. If the water is hot, the rice will start to expand and become starchy before its moment of glory. If the rice is soaked, it will surrender its nutrients to the water and not to you. Also, a crust often forms on the bottom of a rice cooking pot, but I just accept it as one of those things. A heavy castiron pot helps prevent this. Okay now . . .

Wash under cold running water

    2 cups brown rice

Stir it into

    5½ cups vigorously boiling water

To which (optional) you may have added

        A bouillon cube or a teaspoon of broth powder (healthful, one hopes)

        A lump of butter

And

    1 scant teaspoon salt

(Of course, if you flavor rice and if there's any left over you will not be able to make rice pudding out of it.)

Cover immediately, turn the heat down a little and simmer over low heat about forty-five minutes. When it's apparently done, all the water having seemingly evaporated, uncover it and put it on the *lowest possible heat* and continue cooking it for some ten minutes more. Rice cooked in this manner is a delight—absolutely nonstarchy.

ALTERNATE METHOD:

Brown the rice, after washing, for ten minutes in ½ cup hot oil, then add a cup of boiling water.

One cup of raw rice equals about 3½ cups when cooked, feeding about three to four people.

KASHA

Kasha is a pretty word sounding kind of like a Russian peasant girl (with sister Natasha?) whereas "groat," the other name for this, is a hard sound, ugly.

Break into a bowl

An egg

Stir in

1 cup kasha

Make sure each grain is coated.

Add to

3½ cups boiling water or stock

Cover and cook over low heat thirty-some minutes. Fluff with fork and serve. Or sauté the kasha, either with or without the egg treatment, in ¼ cup hot fat until well coated and then add the boiling water. Mushrooms, onions, etc., may, of course, be browned with the kasha in the fat.

If the House, as a whole, has a specialty, it is surely this next dish, originally created by Mike and Ronnie. I think all of us could make it with our eyes closed. It is a regular on the breakfast table to use up leftovers or at parties. People ask us all the time for the recipe, which is a pity as there really isn't any, you just do it. You'll see, though, how it's done, and if you can cook at all, no doubt you'll do it.

OUR RICE
(I didn't quite know what to call this)

Heat up
    Some oil
Add, all neatly sliced
    An onion or two
    A green pepper
    Some mushrooms
    Some carrots
    Some celery stalks
The first two ingredients are necessary, the latter three nearly
so. When all the vegetables are well sautéed, add
    A quantity of cooked rice
    Some raisins, gold
    Caraway seeds
    Basil
    Rosemary
    Oregano
    Celery seed
    Thyme
    Some dried chopped apricots
    Some chopped nuts
All of the above should be added pretty generously and all
spices should be crushed between the fingertips before their
addition to bring out their full flavor. Cook the rice, spices, apricots and nuts until quite hot and the flavors are well mixed.
Then add the following cheeses
    Cheddar
    Muenster
    Mozzarella
cut in little bits. Cook till the cheeses melt, stir a very little and
serve quite hot.

Another rice dish, this Puerto Rican, comes from Julia Vasquez, who lives down the street from us. This, along with most of the other Puerto Rican recipes, were gotten through the use of sign language and guesses and pulling stuff out of the shelves to explain what size pot, or what vegetable. Between us (Julia's kids, Dennis and Annette, aided matters somewhat) we got it, except for a few things which there just is no English word for that I know of, such as *ajíes y recao,* needed both here and in Asopao de Pollo.

PUERTO RICAN STYLE BEANS AND RICE

Wash
> 2 cups white or brown rice (we use brown, she uses white)

Bring 4 cups salted water to boil. When it boils, add the rice.

When the water has boiled away, add
> 2 tablespoons lard, oil or butter

Stir well. Let stand.

Pound to a paste in a mortar and pestle
> 1 clove garlic
> ½ green pepper
> ½ an onion
> A few *ajíes y recao*

Fry the above vegetables, mashed, in a little
> Lard, oil or butter (whatever you used in the rice)

Mix together the vegetables, rice and
> 2 cups cooked kidney beans

Season with
> Salt and pepper

Heat through and serve.

breads

_____

All I can tell you about bread baking is that it's not as hard as you probably think. In fact, it's not hard at all. Nobody taught me how to do it, I just learned from a book. And kneading is just like you imagine, just like they show you in cartoons, very natural. People get so turned on because we make much of our own bread, when, really, it's so easy. Little do they know—they could do it themselves. It *does* take a long time to bake bread. You mix it up and knead it and let it rise and punch it down and let it rise again, and maybe again. But except for mixing and possibly kneading, none of these activities take more than a few minutes. So you can go away and do something and then return in a few hours, do whatever it is, punch the dough down or put it in the oven, and go away again. Bread making and writing, for instance, seem very compatible to me. At this very moment I have a batch of whole wheat rolls rising in one of Big Diane's pottery bowls, a brown one, downstairs. It is just after six o'clock in the morning, and I have been typing all night (I seem to be kind of a nocturnal animal—most of this cookbook has been written between midnight and seven or eight o'clock). I needed scissors about half an hour ago, and I'd left ours downstairs where I was making a poster to advertise a party to raise money for Ecology Action East . . . (but *that's* another story). So I went downstairs and just kind of on the spur of the moment decided to mix up a batch of good healthy rolls before I went back up. And then during my coffee breaks (actually, herb tea or milk breaks) I can attend to it, and then in about three hours they will be done, and I will have fresh, hot rolls with my breakfast, and maybe I will even walk to the corner store which will only just be opening, past all the people on their way to school and work, feeling funny and good 'cause it's the end of my day and the beginning of theirs and go in and say hello to Herman, the tall guy at the corner who is always very paternal toward me and thinks I'm funny 'cause I make a lot of jokes and do crazy things like tell a complete stranger not to buy monosodium glutamate because it causes brain damage. . . . And walk home with my purchase, probably some milk and a piece of fruit, maybe a rare, middle-of-the-winter, fourteen-cent peach, because it's Monday morning and we will be all out of everything and Michael will be going shopping today. You see, probably, how nice it all is, being part of all this activity and it being part of me, and the fresh, hot rolls (maybe I should get butter too, we're low on it—there will be enough for me, but other people will want some too with theirs), an intrinsic and somewhat symbolic part of all this. For bread, homemade bread, is a symbolic thing. It's American—it goes with the pioneers and beginnings and family and life itself, and, really, *that's* why people are so turned on to us baking bread—it's that they maybe see *all* these things as unattainable and bread is a symbol of that and of a family we have. I don't know.

A couple of months ago, this guy had some of our bread at some friend's house. He liked it so much he got in touch with us subsequently. He wanted to buy some from us—eight loaves a week. So we (Little Diane and I) said okay. I mean we like to bake bread and spread the word that healthy food really tastes good. And the next week he wanted more—sixteen loaves a week. That really takes a long time to make, especially since Diane got a job the second or third week and that meant I had to do all the work except one or two loaves. It got so we were working *all day long* to turn out those breads. Now, we made them with very fine ingredients. We weren't buying through the Co-op then, so the stuff wasn't organic, but it was *real—*

lots of eggs, butter, healthy oil, good flours, honey. We figured out the costs of the breads, and it was incredible. They
were really high compared with store prices, even for healthy
bread, and this not even counting "profit." It was impossible
to do it. It worked out that I was getting something like *two
dollars* for a *whole day's work,* and I knew, when the gas bill
came that would be even higher and it wasn't figured in. What
could I do? We began cutting down on the quality of the ingredients—regular oil for healthy, margarine or even Crisco
for butter, powdered milk for real milk, and, of course, many
fewer raisins and nuts. Some of these ingredients, as you can
see, aren't bad—others are. I couldn't stand it after a week so
I told our bread person what had been going on. I mean, we
labeled all the breads, with ingredients and everything, but he
just didn't seem to know. So we told him about how expensive
it was and how hard it was to even break even and have the
breads be healthy. And he agreed to pay us some two dollars
an hour *plus* the cost of whatever ingredients we used and
thought were best and healthiest. That was fine with me—I
mean two dollars an hour isn't worth much in New York, but
I like to bake bread and be at home, so it was good. The trouble was, that way, it came out to something like twelve dollars
for six loaves of bread. Which is really absurd, and so we
agreed to just stop doing the whole thing. But there you have
another step in the radicalizing of one more person—burnt
irrevocably and emotionally (as opposed to intellectually,
which she knew all along) into her brain is now the leg-
end: *Capitalism can't work.* It's true, it's really true. It's impossible to make good, healthy bread at any kind of profit. Even
allowing for ingredients being much cheaper in bulk, I just
don't see how it can be done. Besides, if you got them in bulk
enough to make it sizably cheaper, you'd be doing so much
business, probably, that you would be shipping the breads all
over the place—and then you'd have to add preservatives or
have stale bread! I really believe the answer lies in small communities. But—and this is what brought all this to mind—it's
interesting that good bread, the symbol of the American dream
(or rather, one of many symbols) cannot be produced within

it, now. I don't consider myself, really, in it. I don't mean that as arrogantly as it sounds—I just mean that I and the people I live with are surely not typical of Americans, and the bread we bake we don't "produce." Some people and their narrow definitions of politics! Baking a loaf of brown bread in this society is revolutionary, if you know why you're doing it. It is for us.

It also tastes good and helps keep you well. Here are our favorite recipes.

BASIC WHOLE WHEAT BREAD

Soften
> 1 packet or tablespoon yeast

In
> ⅓ cup lukewarm liquid

Combine
> 3 cups liquid
> 1-4 tablespoons shortening
> 2-4 tablespoons sweetener
> 1 tablespoon salt
> 3 tablespoons nutritional yeast

When lukewarm, combine with the yeast mixture and 6 cups whole wheat flour and knead thoroughly, 5-10 minutes, using additional flour if necessary. Place in a greased bowl and cover with a towel. Let rise in a warm place, free of drafts, till about double in bulk. Divide in two, form into loaves and let rise in greased loaf pans till slightly less than double in bulk, and bake at 350°F. for 1 hour.

LIQUID: Use water, milk, orange or even tomato juice, sour cream, sour milk, soup stock or vegetable cooking water. Anything will do, provided it is first heated to lukewarm so the yeast beasties will thrive in it. Milk must be scalded first and then cooled to lukewarm for it contains a bacteria which may affect yeast adversely if not scalded.

SWEETENER: Honey, molasses, sugar, brown sugar, maple syrup.

SHORTENING: Oil, butter, bacon fat (in some breads).

VARIATIONS

Add two beaten eggs to cooled scalded milk and use additional flour. Honey is a good sweetener with this.

Add raisins, chopped nuts, and cinnamon.

Add grated cheese, herbs, spices, anything you like.

Add cracked wheat or other grain soaked in milk or water, or cooked, or any leftover porridge or mashed potatoes.

RYE BREAD: Use sour milk for liquid, molasses for sweetener, add 2-4 tablespoons caraway seed. For flour use 3 cups whole wheat, 1 cup gluten flour, 1½ cups rye flour, ¼-½ cups soy flour. Bake at 300°F. for 2 hours.

ROLLS: Use ⅓ cup shortening. After first rising, form into small balls, let rise in muffin tin (cloverleaf—3 balls per muffin hole). Let rise again, and bake at 400°F. 15-20 minutes. Use milk as liquid.

FOR SHINY TOPS: Brush with beaten egg before baking, melted butter after.

LITTLE DIANE'S RYE BREAD

This bread has good flavor but is quite heavy. To make it lighter, use little or no soy flour and add gluten flour instead.

Dissolve

>   2 tablespoons yeast

In

>   3 cups lukewarm water

Add

>   ¼ cup sweet or sour milk, buttermilk, sour cream, yogurt, scalded and cooled (the buttermilk will curdle when heated but ignore it—it doesn't hurt the bread)
>
>   4 tablespoons brown sugar
>
>   2 tablespoons blackstrap molasses
>
>   ½-1 tablespoon caraway seeds

Blend together and then add, stirring and beating

2 cups dark rye flour
4½ cups whole wheat flour
½ cup soy flour

Let rise, covered, away from drafts, for an hour or so. Turn out onto lightly floured board, shape into loaves and place in greased or liquid lecithined pans. Bake one hour at 350°F.

The following recipe is my own and it's quite rich and very, very good with butter and expensive—because it uses butter in it, and nuts, and raisins, and eggs and cinnamon and everything. This reminds me of the time Big Diane was high, sitting in the kitchen, watching me running around cooking. She started laughing, and laughing as I put nuts and spices and flour and fruit into whatever it was I was making, and she said, "Now I know why everything you make tastes so good! Everything you put in it is good!"

CINNAMON RAISIN BREAD

In a small bowl, dissolve
      2 tablespoons active dry yeast or the equivalent of fresh
In
      ¼ cup lukewarm water
Let stand while you scald
      1⅓ cups milk
Pour the hot milk over
      ¼ cup raw sugar
      2 teaspoons salt
      ½ cup melted butter or margarine
Beat to cool; when lukewarm beat in the yeast mixture and
      3-4 eggs
      2½ cups whole wheat flour
Blend well, then beat in

Another 2½ cups whole wheat flour, or enough to
make a soft dough

Roll out on pastry cloth or lightly floured board. Divide
into two or three sections and spread with

melted butter
cinnamon and sugar
raisins
chopped nuts

Roll each section up tightly and place in greased bread
pan. Brush the top with a little melted butter or margarine. Let
dough rise until doubled again—about forty-five minutes. Bake
at 350 for half an hour.

PASTRY

Also under the heading of breads come various pastries
using yeast to rise. One of the simplest ways to make a coffee
cake is to use the recipe for rolls (page 130), or even a plain
bread recipe. Make half of it into rolls and roll the other half
out fairly thin, after the first rising. Dot the surface thereon
with butter, chopped nuts, and cinnamon. Meanwhile, cook
any kind or quantity of dried fruit in water until soft, and then
squish it up. Add sugar or honey if you like, or any spices that
take your fancy. Spread this mixture over the rolled dough and
roll it up like a jelly roll so that it forms a nice sausage shape.
Put the ends together, forming a ring thereby. If you want to
be fussy about it, glue the ends together by dipping your fin-
ger in a little water. Place on a greased cookie sheet or in any
sort of large round pan (remember, it will rise again), and
then let it rise again, covered by a towel until. Now bake it, at
the temperature prescribed for the rolls, or if it is very big, 25
degrees lower. Bake it until it's golden, and take it out, and
there you are.

Basically another version of pastry is *Danish*. They're
about my favorite thing in the world to eat, but I don't make
them very often 1) because they take a long time and 2) be-

cause they are super costly and 3) because they use far too much butter to be really good for you, even though the home-made variety is certainly far superior to the store bought, nutritionally and of course tastewise. Taste! Let me tell you, Danish are, very possibly, the best thing in the world that I make. I hate to say this, but they even equal Steinberg's Danish, and for those of you who don't know, Steinberg's, a dairy restaurant on the upper West Side, makes pretty damn fine Danish and has been doing so for longer than anyone can remember. And *these* equal *those*. But don't say that I didn't warn you that they take a long time!

INCREDIBLE DANISH

All ingredients should be at room temperature, and I repeat my previous warning: these take a *long* time to make. They're so good, however. Also, this is an extra-large recipe. You might want to cut it in half.

Beat well

> 4 eggs

Add

> 1½ cups lukewarm water (or milk, if you like)

and beat again. Now dissolve in this mixture

> 2 cakes, tablespoons or packages of yeast

Refrigerate this for about 15 minutes while you get the following together.

> 7 cups sifted wholewheat flour
>
> 2 teaspoons salt
>
> 3 tablespoons raw sugar
>
> 1 cup butter (and it's just beginning)
>
> 1 tablespoon powdered cardamom (this is one of its secrets—gives it a lovely smell and a slightly lemony taste)
>
> 1 teaspoon grated lemon or orange rind (optional)

Mix till smooth. The butter must be well incorporated into everything else. Now make a well in the above ingredients and pour in the chilled egg-yeast mixture. Work this in well and knead lightly on a floured board for two minutes. The dough should be light and as soft as a baby's cheek. Form into a smooth ball and refrigerate twenty minutes while you clean up the mess made thus far. (If you don't do it as you go along, it will be really overwhelming by the time you finish.) Now remove the dough from the refrigerator and divide it in two. Roll out very, very lightly into a rectangle ½ inch thick (about). It need not be that thin. Have ready

2 to 3 cups butter, beaten till creamy

Divide this in two, half for each ball of dough, and divide each half into quarters, so you have eight lumps of butter altogether. Dot one of these lumps of butter over one of the sections of dough you've rolled out and then fold it over itself into thirds. Turn dough slightly and roll out again. Repeat butter treatment three times, four times in all, with each ball of dough. Let rise another 2 hours, chilled. Then roll out again, cut into squares, and on each square place a blob of filling (see opposite). Pull two of the corners opposite each other together so that you have a sort of package. Secure, using water as glue. Brush these Danish, after you've made a bunch, with an egg beaten with a little water. Sprinkle with raw sugar to give a pretty sparkle, and a few slivered almonds. Now place on a lightly greased cookie sheet, well apart (for they will rise some more). Bake at 370°F. for about fifteen minutes.

FILLING:

Cook either dried pitted prunes or apricots until thick and soft in a small amount of water. Mash a little and add honey and cinnamon and grated lemon peel to taste.

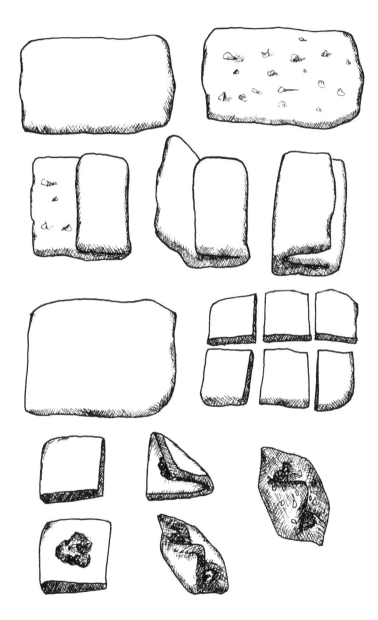

desserts

And that, as far as I can tell, about brings us to desserts and sweets. Personally, I really dig something sweet to finish off a meal with, and I *really* like it if it's healthy. We all kind of feel that way. Most desserts we have are fruit-based ones, fruit being easy to prepare and good. But Little and Big Diane and I often bake something. In the latter case whatever it is is usually enriched with wheat germ, soy grits, or whatever. I prepare a lot of custards, a dessert I really like and one high in protein, too. And Little Diane, who, like me, despises waste, will often help out with some rice pudding when brown rice accumulates in the refrigerator.

FRUIT AND FRUIT DESSERTS

MICHAEL'S DELIGHT

This is *so* simple and just incredibly good. Beat up some cream cheese, either with a wooden spoon or with electric beaters, the latter making it fluffier. Beat in a little of the juice from a can of unsweetened pineapple, enough to give it a smoother texture but not a runny one, and a few vigorous dashes each of cinnamon, nutmeg and ground cloves. Spread this mixture on slices of the pineapple, topping with other slices, or mound it up and top with pineapple chunks. Use the kind that comes in juice as opposed to syrup.

RONNIE'S DELIGHT

One day Ronnie and Dave went shopping and they bought some things that weren't on the list. "We didn't know why," said Ronnie. "The guy looked at us and said, 'You want some strawberries?' and we looked at each other and we said okay." But when they got home, it turned out to be Big Diane's birthday, and with the extra ingredients they invented a dessert that has since become almost staple here.

Mix thoroughly

     A container frozen strawberries

     A few containers of vanilla or plain yogurt

     A large glop of sour cream

     One or two sliced bananas

That's all and it's really good. A variation on this is to just put strawberries and sour cream and a little bit of nutmeg in the blender and whir till smooth.

DAVE'S DELIGHT

Also simple, and of a fruit and dairy product base. Dice apples, bananas and oranges, plus any other fruit you like. Toss with cottage cheese and yogurt.

FRUIT CRUNCH

This is drab looking and plain but really good, one of my old standby-type desserts. Actually, it is less a crunch than a squish.

Combine till crumbly
>   ¾ cup soft butter
>   ¼-½ cup brown sugar
>   ½ cup whole wheat flour
>   ½ cup wheat germ
>   ½ cup soy grits

Put a little less than half of this mixture into a greased pan and pat well. Put over that

>   Fruit (sliced apples—good tart ones) or peaches or canned sour cherries (thicken juice with flour in saucepan)

Sprinkle fruit (except cherries) with cinnamon and cover with remaining crumb mixture. Pat as firm as you can and bake at 425°F. 30-40 minutes. Serve warm or cold, with cream, whipped or plain, for dessert or a breakfast pastry. Sesame seeds may replace all or part of the soy grits.

APPLE CRISP

As far as I know, this only works well with apples. I have tried other fruits, but only apples give off enough juice to make it good: soft underneath and crunchy on top.

Core but do not peel, and quarter or cut into eighths
>   4 or 5 large tartish apples

Arrange them in a greased square pan. Sprinkle over them
>   The juice of ½ lemon (unless apples are very sour and flavorful)
>   Cinnamon—about ½ a teaspoon

Crumble together in a mixing bowl with your fingers
>   ½ cup whole wheat flour
>   ¼ cup wheat germ
>   ¼ cup sesame seeds
>   ¼ cup brown sugar
>   ¼ teaspoon salt
>   ¾ stick of butter (a bit less than ½ cup)

Press the crumb mixture down firmly over the apples and bake at 325° for ½ hour.

Big Diane has been into making pies since she moved in, and no doubt earlier too. But they've changed since she moved in. Originally, while tasting good and looking pretty, they were quite unhealthy, using white sugar and flour and Crisco in the crust. Her first experiments at bettering them were a flop. You can't simply substitute whole wheat for white flour, for instance, and have it turn out—you need less. And so on. But now she has evolved to absolutely the most outasite pies you can imagine. Her apple pie, in particular, is absolutely unbeatable. Others prefer her pumpkin, her cherry, her blueberry, but apple is what I like. And, no matter how hard I try, I just can't seem to get into making pies successfully, not the fillings as much as the crust. This crust recipe is the greatest. A whole wheat crust has some substance and taste between your teeth instead of just dissolving into paste.

BIG DIANE'S WHOLE WHEAT CRUST

Sift together
>   3 cups whole wheat flour
>   2 teaspoons salt

Cut in
>   1½ cups butter, slightly softened
>   1¼ cups wheat germ

When crumbly, add gradually
>   About ½ cup cold or ice water

Knead just barely enough so dough will be rollable and divide in fourths (this recipe is for two double crusts or four single ones). Slightly more dough should be used for bottom crusts. Turn rolled dough into pan, fill and bake (*see* Fillings) or bake at 425°F. for eight minutes.

FILLINGS:

APPLE PIE
Slice apples and core but do not peel. Use good tart firm ones. Toss with 1 tablespoon sugar or honey, or to taste, 1-2

tablespoons flour, 1 teaspoon cinnamon, a fleck black pepper, a little cloves and nutmeg. Add lemon juice if apples are not tart enough. Put on top crust.

PEACH PIE

Slice but do not peel fresh peaches. Remove pits (obviously). Toss slices with 1 tablespoon sugar, ½ teaspoon cinnamon, 1 tablespoon flour, a little lemon juice. Put on top crust. When heat is lowered, brush top with beaten egg and 15 minutes before pie is done sprinkle with sugar for a glazed effect.

Bake pies at 425°F. ten minutes and 325°F. half an hour.

Little Diane and I stick to other dessert bakings, namely cookies and cakes. Both get baked and/or frozen weeks ahead whenever there is an event coming up. A sign goes up on the refrigerator door—stuff baked for Ecology Party (wedding, Earth Day, whatever). We always make the same things, just about. (I survey the list and say to her: *Aha!* I see you beat me to sesame oatmeal crisps this time!) Some come from the *Natural Foods Cookbook,* but most we have invented or revised from other cookbooks. My favorite types are bar cookies, that is, those baked in a square pan and sliced after cooling, and refrigerator cookies, that is, those in which the dough is mixed up, formed into a sausage shape, sliced and baked later. Both of these are easy types. Although drop cookies are not *much* trouble, they are *more* trouble and so I usually leave them for Little Diane to do. She doesn't seem to mind. Both of us, however, shy away from rolled-out cookies although they really aren't difficult if a pastry cloth is used. Of course, then you have to clean the pastry cloth! Well, go please everybody.

WHEAT GERM BROWNIES
(My very favorites)

Combine in this order
    ¼ cup oil
    1 egg

1 tablespoon molasses

½ cup honey

2 teaspoons vanilla or 1 teaspoon each vanilla and
   cinnamon

1 cup wheat germ

¼ teaspoon salt

½ cup noninstant milk powder

1-3 tablespoons nutritional yeast

Blend well and add

¼-½ cup each chopped walnuts and/or raisins

Spread in a well-greased pan and bake at 350°F. for half
an hour.

Some brands of carob powder (which is a chocolate substitute made from the powdered fruit of the tamarind) taste
exactly like chocolate, others don't. We recommend the El
Molino cara-coa.

CAROB BROWNIES

Melt

⅓ cup butter

Stir in

⅓ cup carob powder

½-1 cup raw sugar

1-2 eggs (use a smaller pan if one egg is used)

½ cup whole wheat flour

¼ cup wheat germ

½-1 cup chopped nut pieces

1 teaspoon vanilla

½ teaspoon salt

Bake at 325°F. half an hour. Makes one pan—about nine
good-sized brownies.

SURPRISING BROWNIES: Add additional nuts, some raisins,
and coconut.

TAHINI COOKIES

Cream together
>½ cup each butter and honey
>2 tablespoons molasses
>1 cup tahini (ground sesame-seed butter) or a mixture of nonhydrogenated unsweetened peanut butter and tahini or all peanut butter

When smooth, add, stirring after each addition
>1 cup wheat germ
>1 teaspoon vanilla
>¼ teaspoon each cinnamon and ginger
>¾ teaspoon salt
>1 cup milk powder
>½ cup whole wheat flour

Sprinkle a large piece of waxed paper generously with
>Sesame seeds

Place the dough, formed into a sausage shape, on it. Roll dough in paper and chill well. Remove paper. Slice and bake at 350°F. 8-10 minutes on a well-greased cookie sheet.

CAROB MACAROON PUFFS

Cream together
>1 cup dark brown raw sugar (or a bit less)
>½ cup oil

Add and beat well
>2 egg yolks
>¼ cup milk

Mix together and stir in
>1 cup whole wheat flour
>3 tablespoons carob powder
>¼ cup wheat germ
>1¼ cups oats, or a bit less
>1 teaspoon cinnamon
>Dash nutmeg

1 cup coconut meal

Beat until stiff

2 egg whites

Fold them gently but thoroughly into the batter, along with

1 teaspoon vanilla

½ teaspoon almond extract

Drop by teaspoonfuls onto a well-greased cookie sheet and bake at 350°F. for about ten minutes.

We're all great cheesecake fans, and every two months or so one of us gets it together to make one, even though they're expensive. They vary, depending on who's the creator—either Big Diane, Michael, or me, but they're all similar—incredible.

CRESCENT'S CHEESECAKE

This is a basic cheesecake recipe. Place in the blender in this order

2 eggs

¼ cup cottage cheese

8 ounces cream cheese

½ cup honey or raw sugar, light or dark

¼ cup noninstant milk powder

2 teaspoons vanilla

1 teaspoon almond extract

1 small chunk lemon, with rind

Pour into crumb crust. Place in a pan of boiling water and bake at 300°F. for about 25 minutes, or until middle does not shake.

TOPPING

Mix together the following:

1 cup yogurt or sour cream

¼ cup sugar, or less

A little vanilla

A teaspoon or so ground cinnamon and a little nutmeg
Spread carefully over the top of the cake and bake another ten minutes.

I prefer this chilled rather than warm, though of course it can be eaten either way, but I usually can't wait. This recipe is also rather small in quantity but quite rich—it will give five people each a pretty good-sized piece. I vary it each time I make it. My favorite version of it is chilled with frozen or fresh-sliced and stewed strawberries over the top. I also am fond of making it into a fresh-fruit cheesecake: that is, after the sour cream topping has baked five minutes, I remove it from the oven and carefully press into it, arranging them attractively, halved strawberries, fresh pineapple chunks, fresh slices of peaches. The fresh fruit somewhat offsets the richness of the cake and makes a wonderful combination, especially when (variation number three) the cottage cheese has been decreased to an eighth of a cup. If I'm out of sour cream, or wish a particularly picturesque topping, I'm liable to open a can of either pineapple rings in juice or sour pie cherries, drain the juice, reserving the fruit, and mix the juice with a tablespoon or less of cornstarch. I heat it on the stove over medium heat for about five minutes, or until clear and lightly thickened. When I take the cheesecake from the oven, minus sour cream, at the end of the twenty-five minutes, I arrange the pineapple slices on top, sprinkle with cinnamon and pour the thickened juice over. Cherries are added after the juice has been poured and sprinkled lightly with sugar and nutmeg. And the other variations that I do are not original but belong to other people. Cheesecake certainly is good!

MICHAEL'S CHEESECAKE

Separate the eggs. Place the yolks in the blender along with the other ingredients *except* substitute honey for sugar, omit milk powder and almond extract, use less cottage cheese and add a larger slice of whole lemon, 2 tablespoons soy flour, one or two tablespoons grated sharp cheddar, and, occasionally, a large handful of any variety of nuts (almonds are nice) or seeds, pumpkin or sunflower. When batter is blended, whip the egg whites stiff—this must be done by hand or electric mixer, the blender will *not* do it—and fold them into it. Bake the same period of time as Crescent s Cheesecake and use the sour cream topping.

BIG DIANE'S CHEESECAKE

Follow the basic recipe, omitting lemon and using sugar instead of honey. After batter has been whooshed in the blender, fold in one cup heavy cream, which has been whipped. Bake as directed, and use sour cream topping, omitting cinnamon and nutmeg and using instead ginger and additional sugar for flavoring. Serve, if possible, with fresh blueberries.

PLAIN OLD CUSTARD

Don't ever really make this plain though, or not more than once or twice, or you'll get sick of it which would be a shame, it being a high-protein and really tasty dish.

Beat together till smooth

> 4-6 tablespoons raw sugar or a bit more of honey
> ¾ cup noninstant milk powder
> ¾ cup milk
> 4 eggs
> 1-3 teaspoons soy flour
> 1 tablespoon (or less if you're not used to it) nutritional yeast
> 1½ teaspoons vanilla
> Pinch salt

When smooth (a wire whisk is good to use here) add and beat well

> 2 cups milk

Pour into greased custard cups or a shallow greased pan (a deep casserole doesn't work because then the custard doesn't get done in the middle) and sprinkle with

Nutmeg or cinnamon

Place the cups or pan in a larger pan of water. Bake in a steamy oven (this is what the water does) for forty minutes to an hour (*maybe*) or until a knife inserted in the center of the custard comes out clean and the middle does not shake with liquid. If it was baked in a shallow square pan, such as a brownie pan, cut into squares and serve. Plain, it's good on a plain-type cake, sliced and toasted slightly, or with crispy cookies, or with fresh or stewed fruit (raspberries are nice) over it. Vary it by using orange extract instead of vanilla, adding a grated orange rind (but only organic) and a tablespoon or so of frozen orange-juice concentrate, if you have it. This is really orangey and good.

VARIATIONS:

Coconut custard may be prepared by making up coconut milk (page 85 under chicken curry) and using it instead of regular milk in the above recipe. Sprinkle, after cooking, with more coconut (use coconut meal, the grated organic sugarless dry kind, from Pete's Spice—*see* Where to Shop) and brown prettily under the broiler. Or turn it into tropical custard which has been made with coconut milk, *and* a tablespoon of orange juice or concentrate and half a mashed banana added to the mixture. When baked, give it the broiled coconut-meal treatment, chill well, and garnish with banana slices, and serve. You may add chopped almonds to either tropical or plain custard and turn plain custard into almond custard if along with the almonds you add almond extract (whew!). Fruit custard is yours by adding any chopped fruit, fresh, canned and drained or dried, to the custard along with a little bit of freshly grated ginger or crystallized ginger. Any custard can be glazed after completion by sprinkling with raw sugar and running under a hot broiler for a moment. Or you can give up on the idea of custard altogether, and use up your leftover brown rice in one noble motion, by making

DIANE'S LEMON RICE PUDDING

Blend till smooth
> 4 eggs
> ½ teaspoon each vanilla and lemon extract
> ½ cup raw sugar
> ½ cup milk powder
> ½ teaspoon salt

Stir in
> 3½ cups each milk and cooked brown rice
> Juice and rind of 1 lemon

Turn into a well-greased baking dish, bake at 325°F. half an hour.

Baking powder and soda, used to leaven cakes, cookies and muffins, have the unfortunate side effect of neutralizing various vitamins, soda to a greater extent than powder, which is why you find neither used here. You would think, then, that our cakes, if indeed we had cakes, would be quite heavy, but this is really not the case. Eggs are used as leavening, the yolks and whites being separated, and the whites beaten to peaks and then folded in at the last. However, this process is a lot of trouble and expensive to boot, so most often we foreswear cakes. Here are the exceptions to the rule.

BROOKLYN CAKES
(and variations)

Separate
> 4 eggs

Beat the yolks till thick with
> 2 teaspoons vanilla

Beat in gradually
> 1-1½ cups raw sugar

Sift in
>1¾ heaping cups sifted whole wheat flour
>½ teaspoon salt

Heat together till the butter melts
>1 cup milk
>2-4 tablespoons butter

Stir into egg–sugar mixture and beat till smooth. Whip the egg whites till stiff, fold them in and bake at 350°F. 30-35 minutes, or until toothpick comes out clean.

TROPICAKE:

Add a couple of mashed bananas to batter before egg whites are folded in. Immediately after cake is baked spread with orange marmalade.

Sprinkle with coconut meal.

Add chopped nuts to cake, and/or cinnamon.

Top with the following:

BROILED FROSTING

Mix and spread on cakes
>¼ cup butter
>¼ cup brown sugar
>¼ cup cream or evaporated milk
>½-1 cup chopped nuts and/or coconut meal

Broil till brown.

This frosting is good on Oatmeal Cake, too.

OATMEAL CAKE

Over
>1 cup oatmeal
>½ cup wheat germ

Pour
>1½ cups boiling water

Let stand half an hour.

Meanwhile, cream together
>   ¾ cup butter
>   1-1½ cups brown sugar

Beat in
>   2 eggs
>   1½ teaspoons vanilla

Sift in
>   1¼ cups whole wheat flour
>   ½ cup noninstant milk powder
>   ¾ teaspoon salt
>   Cinnamon, nutmeg, ginger to taste
>   1 tablespoon nutritional yeast

and beat in the softened oats and wheat germ. Bake at 350°F. just short of an hour and broil with frosting as above.

I really don't enjoy most substances relegated to the position of candies and confections. But the following are for those with a sweet tooth.

UNCOOKED CANDIES

Combine
>   2 parts peanut butter
>   ¼-½ parts mild honey
>   1-3 teaspoons vanilla

That is our base. Now add any of the things in List One to make a creamy consistency, rollable into little balls. Add anything from List Two for flavor and variety in texture (this may be omitted if you want a smooth confection) and roll into little balls. Dip the balls into anything from List Three.

LIST ONE
>   Milk powder
>   Wheat germ
>   Nutritional yeast

      Carob powder

      Soy flour

LIST TWO

      Chopped nuts, any variety

      Raisins

      Coconut meal

      Bone meal

      Oatmeal

      Any crisp cereal (crunchy Granola?)

LIST THREE

      Coconut meal

      Sesame seeds

      Soy grits

      Ground nuts

For a particularly delicious taste, sort of caramel-fudgey, use lots of carob powder, a little milk powder, some wheat germ.

OTHER VARIATIONS:

Use cashew, almond or other nut butter to replace peanut butter.

Use molasses to replace honey.

Use any extract other than vanilla.

Tahini (ground sesame seed butter) may also replace peanut butter—add some pistachio nuts—and you've got mock halvah!

———————

No cookbook for and about groups of us living together would be complete without some mention of the scarfies, alternately called the munchies, the blind munchies, or the hungry grundies: that strange desire occurring anywhere from immediately to an hour or two after smoking dope; that desire that sneaks up behind you and hits you over the head and says *Food*.

Things generally, it must be remembered, are much more intense when one is stoned; food is anything but an exception. The cravings and hungers that arise are like at no other time; they demand fulfillment. At one time in my life I lived near a bakery that was open all day, closed about five in the evening and opened again after midnight. At night, you'd go in the back out of the dark and into a floury white bright sweet-smelling hub of activity: bakers running around, sliding bread in and out of ovens, knotting crullers like automatons. You'd blink in the brightness, coming in from the quiet city and breathe deeply. You'd walk around dazzled by the choice of delights, hot from the oven, get higher than you were already on the fragrance. Maybe you'd go there with a couple of friends, maybe not; often your eyes would be red from staying up late reading; most times you'd be stoned out totally—why else would an urge for a greasy, sugary, warm Pratzael doughnut come on you like a visiting spirit? So you go in there—and there are five or ten of your friends, scarfing doughnuts in the brightness, laughing, completely spaced out, riffing off each other and the bakers, the same urge having come on them, and there you all are. . . .

There is no need, though, to eat unhealthy food, to go out to Pratzael's or your neighborhood gathering place, unless you just dig the change in environment. Get it together and go into the kitchen and fix something for you and all your friends.

What should it be? Well, once you get together the energy to overcome the inertia and make it into the kitchen, you'll find moving around and combining things and slicing and chopping to be even more enjoyable and intense than usual. It might take you longer to fix something: you'll get hung up on the way that eggplant feels, or stare for a few minutes at the cut inside a red cabbage. Or maybe you'll find a carrot or a stalk of celery humorous for some reason or another and take a moment to laugh. But sooner or later you'll get down to it and prepare something absolutely incredible.

Incredible doesn't mean elaborate. What comes out of my mind and kitchen most often is something like the appetizer plate described at the beginning of the chapter Appetizers. It's important for me to bear in my mind what you should always bear in mind when cooking: that diversity and contrast are the key things. Contrast colors: golden cheese, brown caraway seeds, green parsley, and/or textures: soft cottage cheese and crisp celery. And/or temperature: chilled juice and hot melted cheese on crackers. Oh, you'll have a great time doing it, really. And your friends will just flip out.

Remember: if it's good when you're straight, it's probably better when you're stoned. Or, no, that isn't quite true. I can still sometimes eat shit food and have it taste OK to me, but when I'm stoned, it almost never does. Plain brown rice is out of sight, stoned. The flavors, like in anything you eat flying high, just leap into your mouth, and the textures are so good! I've had food and hash so good that I've spent fifteen minutes chewing one bite of shrimp curry. I *think* it was fifteen minutes!

A few specific rushes: a piece of icy cold watermelon, seeds and all; fresh fruit, chilled deeply, with soft cheese at room temperature; a soup with all kinds of surprising things in it, an Oriental dish with crispy bits of this and that, a slice of warm pie with a glass of cold milk.

how to live without very much money
(or maybe for free)

For the most part, the answer has to do with getting together with other people (a lot of answers lie therein). Five, ten, twenty or a hundred people can live together much more cheaply as a unit than as individuals, whether in the city or country. Part of it is simply the way things are set up (large quantities are more economical), but it goes far beyond that. Recently the Alternate U people drove down to the industrial district, to a cheese outlet, and got three *huge* boxes of cheese *free*. Apparently, the manufacturer opens the boxes of cheese before shipping them, and if they have *one little spot of mold* —in a whole big fifty or so pound box—they throw it out. And then it goes to us! But only if we get together. What would one person *do* with two hundred and fifty pounds of cheese? And how would he or she get it? Or know about it? Anyway, I'm not kidding, capitalism wastes so much. In its waste lie the seeds of its destruction, but also the possibility of our survival *now*. We need to learn to get together, to find out where the system dumps its garbage—and steal it! (Our house is furnished

153

with milk crates—the kind of a sturdy wooden nature found all over the city.) And, we need to share our knowledge. *Fuck the System*, a survival manual widely circulated on the Lower East Side a couple of years ago, has a lot of such helpful household hints, but unfortunately is out of date now. As I say, find out your own. Some of ours follow.

Our thing to do is to liberate stuff you need, or even sometimes, stuff you don't. Alternatively called stealing, lifting, or ripping off, I like the somewhat more optimistic name for this practice—liberating. If you want to get into this, and you should, examine yourself closely. Raise your consciousness. Question your views of morality. I honestly believe that if I need something it should be mine, or my family's, and that I shouldn't have to pay for it. I honestly believe that when I go into nearly any store and pay for something *I* am being ripped off. The price farmers get for beef cattle is between 24 and 34 cents per pound on the hoof, between 48 and 68 cents a pound dressed, approximately the same price they got in 1949. When I go into a New York City Store for nonorganic meat, I almost never pay under a dollar for nonfatty meat and much more for the so-called good meats. (So-called because virtually *all* supermarket meat, regardless of cut, has been contaminated by the antibiotics, tranquilizers and artificial hormones routinely given animals raised for food.) The more expensive tender cuts range anywhere from a dollar-fifty to two dollars, two-fifty, and even upwards of that sometimes. Now the difference between what *I* pay and what the farmer gets sure as hell goes somewhere. Shipping, wages, packaging (non-biodegradable!) don't take any seventy-five cents, eighty-five cents, a dollar-thirty per *pound* of beef. That money goes somewhere, to someone, and you can bet that someone doesn't ever have to think about being able to afford or not afford certain cuts of beef, or number of servings per pound. I think about all this and more, about all the gimmicks to get you to buy, all the useless packaging designed to attract or conceal the fact that there is little inside, and, in fact, all the useless possessions that we have been taught to want to pile up in order to be happy. And I get furious, I get mad, seeing stores profit off the very insecurities and fears they have created in people, and *I* force myself to steal, and my heart pounds very fast because of course I am still afraid, of course I am not free from indoctrination, of course, I, like all of us, have been programmed to police myself. And thus, I find "stealing" to truly be liberating and not stealing at all—liberating not only of goods but of *myself*. I learn in my emotions what I know in my head—that the system is an emperor's new clothes, that the system is a paper tiger, that the system exists only because we believe in it and if we cease to it falls apart. Security devices, security cops are mostly to convince you that you can't get away with it. You can! You can get away with anything if you believe it, almost. Getting caught is like being dropped on by a bird. It happens, but it ain't too likely. This is not to say don't be cool—of course you should—be aware of two-way mirrors and electrical price tags and stuff hidden in books. But don't let it stop you. Your belief is your main weapon. I *really believe* that I should be able to ride the subways free, do anything I want without paying for it, be able to smoke dope anytime and anywhere, and I will. I *really believe* there will be a resolution, and there will, but for that one, a whole *lot* of people have to believe. At any rate, don't worry about getting caught. And if you do, you do. I guess it's the risks of the profession. But, from all the people I know who do it, and the tiny percentage who have gotten caught, they are hardly ever prosecuted. I haven't been caught yet, but if I do I know I'll slip chameleon-like into a role Penitent. Crying Female. Giddy Socialite. First-time teen-ager. I'll use their own sexism against them to survive, and I will. I *know* I'll be okay. Looking back over this section, I see there's one thing I haven't gone into at all, because it seems almost self-evident to me, and that is, of *course*, you don't steal from your brothers and sisters. And even something more: although anyone who has a store is going to be into making money to some extent, some people really try and give you a fair deal, at relatively less exploitative prices or really superior quality. Or they deal with you personally, and they trust you, and those people you don't rip off because they don't rip you off. It's this impersonal, *super-*exploitative shit that bothers me, and, I suspect, most people, as supermarkets and department stores generally have the heaviest security things and are ripped off most often. I never rip off things around the corner and I won't at any country grocery store where people treat you like a human being.

Okay now, two other things about liberating stuff and then onwards. Number One is a specific suggestion. Number Two is a funny story. Number One: Susan goes shopping with Levy, her year-old son. She pushes him in his carriage. She takes a package of shell steak here: she puts it under the carriage. She adds some frozen orange juice, some milk, some tuna. When she fills up the rack *under* the carriage, see her drop the deviled ham into the bag *behind* the carriage. The butter. The vanilla extract (pure). See Susan and Levy stroll over toward the checkout counter. See Susan remove two or three items from the carriage bag, place them on the counter, pay for them, bag them, and meander away, with an *almost* free dinner. See Susan say, "I did that for about seven months and nothing ever happened." Number Two. Once I was working in a health-food store where I was that shamelessly underpaid. I demanded either part-time work or a better salary. I was fired. On that day I went around the store, merrily plucking this and that and dropping it into my large brown bag. I specifically picked a bottle of super expensive ginseng (a root which is supposed to have incredible rejuvenating powers) and royal jelly pearls for my mother who was feeling a bit under the weather. But when I gave it to her and told her the story, she said, "It was very sweet of you to steal it for me, Crescent, but I . . ." Okay—some hints.

If you are a commune and I haven't talked you into organic food co-ops, or if you can't afford it, find the local wholesale fruit and vegetable market. The one nearest us is called *Hunts Point Terminal Market,* and it's really ugly, but you sure can get cheap vegetables there. What you do is first you get in touch with several other communes, also nonorganic eating. Each commune puts in somewhere around five, ten, fifteen dollars. One morning, a person from each participating commune goes up there, all together with some idea of what his or her group wants. You then purchase the food, for absolutely incredible prices. Crates of one hundred oranges for $3.50, bags of onions for $2.75, of cabbages for $2.50, of potatoes for $1.75!

Obviously, this remarkable bargain cannot be taken advantage of by individuals, or even by small groups. What would a couple of people *do* with fifty pounds of cabbage? Just another example of how mutual aid works. Although we were only involved with a vegetable market shopping group in our pre-co-op days, I'm sure every large city has dairy and meat markets that could be worthwhile to investigate. And, most probably a group could get a wholesaler's license and buy canned goods and the like at cost, in quantity. What does a 6,000 pound soybean say? *Cheap!!*

Somehow, the "economy cooking" sections in various cookbooks all seem the same—beginning and ending with chili con carne and having a variety of ground beef and macaroni dishes in between, none very healthful or original or different tasting. One problem is America is too hung up on having meat every night. When you're broke, become a vegetarian. Some people say it's healthier and with a little knowledge of nutrition it can certainly be *as* healthy. The one thing not to do is to start eating all starches and no protein, i.e., spaghetti again. Soybeans are a legume, the *only* legume which supplies protein that breaks down in a meat-like way in the body. Their virtues are extolled further and recipes are given for them in the soybean section. Nuts, another nonanimal source of protein, are expensive shelled, often more so than meat, but they contain no waste whatsoever and hence turn out to be an economical buy. However, not all varieties contain complete protein. (A complete protein is one containing all eight of the 22 amino acids that cannot be synthesized in the body necessary to build health.) As far as I can tell from scanning protein charts, pecans have none, and almonds, cashews, peanuts and sunflower seeds have complete protein. But I'm not positive. Some of them are borderline, as peanuts can "support growth and maintenance but not reproduction" (Adelle Davis, *Let's Eat Right to Keep Fit*).

Eggs are among the highest quality protein food there is

and are cheap too. Soufflés are *really* cheap, because as the egg whites are whipped to a greater volume there is more in terms of bulk than if you were just eating them scrambled. You eat only one or one and a half eggs instead of three or four. Soufflés are also really good.

Fish, too, is very cheap, especially for the lesser-known varieties. Although recent findings about mercury pollution have shown fish not to be as healthy as once was thought, they are still relatively organic, usually having been caught rather than raised. They may have been treated with nitrates, but they just as well may not have been. Look for glossy eyes, bulging as if fresh caught. Shellfish are often more expensive than meat. The shells of bivalves should not be open when bought, in any case.

And don't forget organ meats, good, super healthful and, while slightly more costly than eggs, fish or soybeans, certainly well below tenderloin. Recipes for them are on page 68. And last, if you stick to all vegetable soybeanless dishes, enrich them with the cheap and omnipresent yeast, powdered milk, and wheat germ proteins.

If you live in the country and for some reason do not have your own supply of milk (i.e. a goat or a cow), you will be delighted to find that in most places raw (unpasteurized) milk is cheaper than regular. For those of you who don't know, it tastes *so* much better and has a lot more nutritive value.

A useless and polluting expense is that of dishwashing liquid. If you let things soak, you can almost always scrub them off without too much work. It's just a question of letting them soak long enough. M.F.K. Fisher, has written wisely in *How to Cook a Wolf,* a cookbook of the Depression and war period:

> It is surprising how clean dishes can be, and how effortless the task can be, and how small the soap bill can be, given a small stream of moderately hot water and a stiff brush. With a certain amount of practice your hands, even the one holding the plate or cup, need never be in the water . . . and if you scrape the plates first, which of course you would do, the sink stays clean, the drains stay fresh, and your brush,

which you get free from the Fuller man [note: M.F.K.
Fisher is one of us!], lasts for a boringly long time.

You hold the plate under running water, turn it
with one hand and scrub it with the other, and put it
in a rack on the drain board. When you have collected
a few, you dry them—before they are cold.

This scheme sounds rather dreamy, put down in
cold print, but it works well. . . .

If there is one thing America has a lot of, it is garbage.
Useless packaging, designed to attract us, to play on our insecurities and make us think we're getting something which in
reality we're not, piles up everywhere. And it's virtually impossible to get rid of it as it piles. We fill in bays and wetlands with
it—destroy aquatic life and make beach swimming a thing of
the past. Paper packaging breaks down relatively easily—but it
uses up forests at an alarming rate.

Trees grown for pulp take about seven years to mature.
Their growth depends largely on the use of artificial fertilizers
which poison the land and water and do not replace trace nutrients necessary for the health of the soil and everything that
grows out of it. They are then cut down and another "crop"
planted, depleting the soil of nutrients over and over again,
taking out but not putting back in. Plastics made from synthetic
materials are even more insidious in some ways. Polyvinyl, a
versatile and often used plastic (Saran wrap is a polyvinyl)
produces phosgene gas when burned, a poisonous gas used
during World War I. Why should *we* contribute to this shit?

The House, having eaten organic food for a few months,
decided to try living organically for awhile. We began using a
minimum of plastics and reusing all plastics and tin foil. We
separated out garbage and buried orange peels, banana skins,
leftovers and anything breakdownable in the backyard. It has
worked out well, although, of course, it does take work and
time. But better a sore muscle than a whiff of phosgene gas!
("Exposure for only a short duration to 50 parts phosgene per
million parts air will cause death." *Ramparts,* May 1970, "The
Making Of A Pollution Industrial Complex" by Martin Gellen).
At least, as far as I'm concerned. The new society isn't going to

waste *any*thing, and we should start living it now as much as we can. We have to take it upon ourselves personally not to make huge amounts of garbage, not to use nonbiodegradable detergents or detergents with phosphates.

But, and this is the "but" that 99 percent of the ecology literature seems to forget, we should never forget that *we* are not the ones who caused air pollution or water pollution. *We* are only the people, tiny individuals who had no options open: either we eat food wrapped in ten layers of cellophane or we don't eat food. Either we drive in a car forty miles on the freeway to work or we don't work. We should never forget that picking up candy wrappers is ultimately useless and absurd and doesn't stop pollution. But when individuals come together, they make all-powerful groups that can and will and *are* creating and demanding *new* options, a way of life that doesn't come *prepackaged* and *individually wrapped,* a new society based on human energies and potentialities of *all* people, not a few, based on ecological precepts, based on never taking away without putting back and *not* based on profit. You don't use *reform* when the world is fucking coming to an end, when there's no getting away from the bad air and bad water, you don't pass laws, you don't keep using words, traveling in circles. You don't cut off the "environmental crisis" from any other crisis. Is Harlem, is Bed-Sty, a *good environment?* Is a war that drags on and on, pretending not to be a war, killing numberless people, a war that stretches and spreads, a *good environment?* Why do we never hear about the ecology of the ghetto, or of Vietnam— that since 1962 nearly *five* MILLION *acres* have been defoliated there, making a desert the size of Massachusetts, destroying "enemy cover" and food crops? You change, you fight, you make revolution in a hurry—you *don't* stop to pick up candy wrappers.

medicine

Modern medicine can be costly, useless and sometimes even harmful. With good nutrition and supplements, disease can often be avoided and/or cured. Next time, before you go running to the doctor or to the medicine cabinet for old prescriptions, try some of the following. None of them can do you harm and will probably do you good and are cheap.

I am sure that people in America, at least, suffer from colds more than any other defined disease. (By that I mean that while many of us are not actually sick, we are not actually well, either.) We have the "nagging backache, aches and pains" that the commercials refer to so casually and we think they're normal. Most of us have insomnia or fatigue, are depressed or are something that we believe implicitly a pill can cure. Look at the number of over-the-counter sleeping pills, wake-up pills, tranquilizers, etc, etc, available in any drugstore. These are not the supplies of a healthy person. Why? I honestly believe it is a direct result of processed foods that do nothing at all, have no nutritional value.

Anyhow, colds. (Of which I have not had *one* since eating well.) The old things your mother probably told you about and did for you have a good basis in truth. Oranges are good, of course, because they have Vitamin C. Liquids are good because they clean you out and vitamins are often better utilized in a liquid. (Chicken soup?) Anyhow, Vitamin C *really* works for colds—enough will dry out your nose with good side effects as well. The thing is, you have to take *massive* doses, and I mean massive. If I wake up in the morning feeling the least bit coldy, I run downstairs and eat something and quickly swallow down about two or three thousand mg. of Vitamin C, with orange juice, if available. It's important to eat first or the vitamins will get washed through your system. Then, every hour through the day, I take five hundred mg. an hour. After every meal I take the morning dosage. No cold!

Case history: Enter Junior, age twelve, with a terrible cold. We exchange greetings and then I comment on his cold and ask what he's doing for it. He says he's taking something but it's not doing any good. I ask him would he take some vitamins for it if I give them to him. He says do they taste bitter and I say no and I'll even take some too. So we sit down and take some vitamins—he takes 14, I take 28, having agreed to take double what he does. (There is, incidentally, *no* overdose of Vitamin C. When you take too much, it is just excreted—you get diarrhea.) By the time we're finished, he's already breathing more clearly. I give him a little bag of them to take home, instructing him to "tell your mother the minute you get in what they are and who gave them to you." Hippies, drugs, etc. I'm taking no chances. A few days later I see Junior and ask him how his cold is. He says his parents have bought a bottle of Vitamin C. I am stunned and delighted! What a triumph!

At any rate, when you are sick and your object is to get well, your method should be to get as much protein into you with as little strain as possible. The best way I know is

ADELLE DAVIS' WONDER MILK

Combine in a blender
    1-2 eggs
    1 tablespoon lecithin
    1 tablespoon mixed nutritional vegetable oils

1½ teaspoon calcium lactate or 4 teaspoons calcium
    gluconate
¼ cup yogurt
When throughly beaten, add
    1 cup milk
    ½ cup nutritional (brewer's) yeast
    ¼ cup noninstant powdered milk
    1 tablespoon liver powder
    ¼ cup each soy flour and raw wheat germ
You may now flavor it with
    Honey
    Mashed bananas
    Mashed pineapple
    Molasses
    Carob powder
    Orange juice concentrate
    Nutmeg
    Grated lemon rind.
Pour from blender into a large pitcher and add
    3 cups milk (the rest of a quart)
Cover and store in refrigerator.

Although this is fantastically healthy and supplies all needed nutrients in one fell swoop, it should be obvious to even the most hardy that it's not the most delicious thing in the world. If you are brave, though, and truly desire health, you will drink it—⅓ to ½ cup at and between each meal. This will help any kind of sickness—colds, anything.

A good deal more pleasant of the brews are the herb teas called by the French "tisanes." There are hundreds of them, each tasting different, and each doing something different. Some can be grown easily, peppermint for example, but all can be bought, organically or not. There are also combination teas.

8 FRAGRANCE TEA
(This is my own invention)

Steep in hot water (a lot) for a few minutes
    2 tablespoons dried rosehips
    2 tablespoons peppermint leaves
    1 teaspoon mallow flowers
    1 teaspoon camomile flowers
    2 teaspoons fo-ti-tieng leaves
    1 stick cinnamon
    1 whole allspice
    3 whole cloves
    Grated rind and juice of an orange
Strain and serve, sweetening to taste with honey, which is also good for colds. Honey mixed with lemon juice is a delicious cough syrup, salve for burned tongues and—salad dressing! It will loosen mucus and help purify the blood. Molasses (blackstrap) is another fine natural cough syrup, as well as a laxative and a good source of the B Vitamins. However most people do not like its taste nearly as well as they do honey.

Apple cider vinegar is another incredible thing. It seems to help every type of malaise in me, particularly sluggishness in the morning. A little in a glass of warm water will wake you right on up, and not just because of its sourness (which I like). What it does is start the blood circulating faster. It, and yogurt, are also very good for stomach ailments, viruses in particular. Both encourage the growth of helpful bacteria and go down on the harmful kind. It, too, is a blood purifier and will help cure chronic infections, cramps, dizziness and headaches.

Modern medicine is particularly exploitative of women. For women there are so many compounds sold for cramps, and other "women's problems." These compounds, like most other modern drugs, do no good whatsoever except in the very short run. In the long run, all drugs, even the seemingly innocent aspirin, increase nutritional needs tremendously. And that's the least of what they do. Read Barbara Semens, *A Doctor's Case*

Against the Pill, to discover what else they do. At any rate, about cramps—they can all be avoided by the judicious use of a little calcium. Take one dicalcium phosphate at each meal every day, and two or three at each meal when you have your period. You will really be amazed. They are especially effective if taken in combination with Vitamin C. Both can be bought over the counter. Apple cider vinegar is also good for cramps, as mentioned earlier. This next—I don't know if it's just because it tastes so good, but warm coconut milk (*see* page 85 under chicken curry) really seems to help me a lot.

Teen-agers are also pretty exploited as a group. They have much spending power statistically and hence are seduced on all sides by those who have only a profit in mind. The average teen-ager's diet is bad, bad, bad—pizza, Coke, chocolate—all have bad effects on the skin. (Avoid greasy foods, nuts, cocoa and wash daily.) But few follow that knowledge. A good diet and an added supplement of Vitamin B-6, pyridoxine, will clear up your skin in a few weeks, if not sooner, and keep it clear. Buy a bottle of Vitamin B-6 tablets, 50 mg, and take 3-6 a day, 1-2 at each meal. A short-term thing to do also is to rub a cut clove of garlic on any particularly stubborn pimples before you go to sleep—they will generally have come to a head in the morning. Also see Facial, page 179—What You Can Do With Food Besides Eat It.

Another scourge with a nutritional base that affects people my age a lot is mononucleosis. Few diseases that don't kill you are as much of a drag to have as mono—and few have as bleak an outlook for cure or even quick recovery. I had it about a year ago before I was into good food. It begins with a bad, bad sore throat and kind of an achey, cross, tired feeling all over. Then comes the swollen glands—swollen to the size of Ping-Pong balls sometimes. You go to the doctor to see what's going on and he takes a blood test. A few days later you hear (over the phone—by now it's a drag to even move from bed) from the doctor that you have mono. Oh, no, moan groan. What can I do for it? Nothing, he says, stay in bed, drink lots of fluid, take an aspirin if you feel really bad. But—how long will it last? Oh, anywhere from two or three weeks to a few months. But what causes it? It's a viral infection—no one is really sure.

It may be a viral infection but it's *caused* by eating unhealthfully, eating too many processed foods that do not fill. You will not believe it—especially those of you who have had it or know someone who has—but a shot of vitamins will rid you of it in *twenty-four hours!* My regular doctor wouldn't give it to me, and neither probably will yours. Dr. Allan Cott, at 303 Lexington Avenue, is the only doctor I know who will—for only five dollars!!! This miracle shot consists of Vitamins C, B-12 and liver.

And to you disbelievers—all I can say it wait till you get mono.

But one more thing, and this I cannot overemphasize. In this section I have been advocating particular vitamins for this and that. But—you can't be *really* healthy unless *all* nutrients are supplied, and there are some sixty of those, and getting too much of one is almost as bad as getting *none* of any. The subject of nutrition is far too wide to be covered here, even if I had all the knowledge. I can only say you should take the time to learn some basic precepts of nutrition, which, once learned, will never be forgotten and always be useful. And you can guess who I advocate—I've been quoting her all through here—Adelle Davis (*see* Bibliography).

in the kitchen

First, how do you stock your kitchen? If you are alone, you will need hardly anything, as single people rarely cook for themselves let alone anything elaborate. But before you even start thinking about moving stuff in, check for cockroaches. If you live in New York, there is, I'd say, a 95 percent chance of your finding them. Their favorite hangouts are around sinks, baseboards, ovens, tiny crevices and crannies. Come in late at night, turn on the light, and watch them run home. Next day, spray. We have found something called Hargate, which is a natural ingredient insecticide made of ground flowers with no DDT. It is harmless to man (at least supposedly, and it seems to be) and really works well. Stay away from other remedies. Cockroaches return after the usual varieties of insecticide are used and you already are exposed to all that poison but feel tempted to spray again. We tried sulphur candles—with no success. The noxious smoke nearly killed us but left the roaches unharmed. Be forewarned—if you don't do anything, one fine day you will wake up to find roach eggs in your pancake flour. Although roach eggs are probably not bad for you, I don't know anyone who knowingly, happily, eats them. Of course, you should have kept your pancake flour in a covered jar, tightly covered, especially after opening it.

If you buy grains or flour in bulk, transfer them immediately when you get home from the store to a large container, bottle or canister. You can get containers every and any where. Go to Klein's or John's Bargain Stores and invest in a few small plastic garbage cans with tightly fitting covers. Go to restaurants and ask them to give you their old mayonnaise jars (restaurant-size are huge), or you can buy those same jars at "Pete's" for twenty cents each, which is still cheaper than the very modern-looking cubic clear or lightly tinted nesting canisters available. Save large potato chip cans (if you don't eat them, get an unhealthy friend who does). Also save jars from coffee, mayonnaise, applesauce, any big ones. Little spice jars are also good to save as you can get the spices themselves far more cheaply at "Pete's" than at the supermarket, by the ounce or ¼ ounce, but you will need jars to put them in when you get home. Lining the shelves with Contact paper, while expensive, is a relatively good invention as it makes the surfaces easier to clean and cuts down slightly on roach espionage.

Keeping your kitchen clean is important, practically as well as psychologically. Besides fitting the hippie image and attracting roaches, a dirty kitchen is, to my way of thinking, very depressing. But when you clean your dishes, don't use steel wool; little feathery hairs rub off and get into your plate and hence into your mouth and into your stomach where they can cause all kinds of dread diseases. Use Rescue pads, scrub cloths, or anything recommended for Teflon.

Teflon is not, in my opinion, what is known in the trade as a good buy. It is impractical, because you have to buy the special plastic utensils that go with it and can't use the metal ones you probably already have. Teflon wears out quickly, losing its stickless properties, even with the best of treatment—the pans themselves are not of good quality. They're also ugly, and not what you could call the least bit organic (cooking in *plastic?*). I'm sure they're unhealthful too, though this is a purely subjective opinion. The best cooking pots in the world, as far as I'm concerned, are those great heavy, cast-iron pots that are really not too expensive and last a lifetime and then some. They come gray, but with constant use they mellow into adult blackness. This is called seasoning, and it can be helped by *drying* the pot *every time* you wash it—never just leaving it to drain—and then rubbing it with oil or a little unsalted shortening. I also like the way they look. I mean, just compare them to the same thing in Teflon. I have also heard that they're healthful to cook in as the food absorbs a little iron, but I don't know whether I believe that or not. Enamelized cast-iron pans are also good.

For relatively little money you can get good, solid, lasting cooking equipment in *huge* sizes from a restaurant supplier, excellent stuff for quantity cooking. Quantity cooking is a subject that I know must be covered in any cookbook professing to pertain to communes, and yet it is one which I approach with great reluctance. I have done it—and found it at best an elusive thing. Actually, I guess part of it depends on your definition of quantity. Personally, I found it only slightly more difficult to cook for twenty people than for five or ten. But up above there it starts getting difficult, and at around fifty, nearly impossible. And yet, as I say: I have done it. I have a healthy respect for myself for doing it, too. I have cooked, on several occasions, for a hundred or a hundred and fifty people. And I have come out of it a bit wiser, having learned, sadly, some lessons. The first is, you just cannot multiply a recipe out by fifteen and have it work. It just won't, although I don't know why. It is a mysterious fact documented in *The Joy of Cooking*, or I would have thought it was just me. You *must* either triple a given recipe five times as opposed to multiplying by fifteen once, or use a recipe written specifically for quantity eating. Where can you get such recipes? There is a cookbook called, unoriginally, *Quantity Recipes,* by Marion Wood and Katherine Harris, put out by the New York State College of Home Economics. I sent away for it—because although I live with a citified eight-to-ten people now, I can easily see myself, in a few years, having to cook regularly (on my week to cook, that is,) for fifty or so work-whetted appetites. The cookbook was a disappointment, for, although it gave excellent advice as far as what equipment to use, number and cost per serving of various things and how to figure it out, the recipes themselves were *most* unhealthy and unappetizing as far as I could tell. However, if you are a large commune, this book would definitely be a helpful tool. Just revise it heavily. One of its biggest problems is that it tries to be economical and does it by "extending" nearly everything with cheap, vitaminless, proteinless starch. This could be changed so easily to remain relatively economical and yet be healthful. Take, for instance, the recipe for Spanish meat loaf given on page 61. Regard the cookbook version and my revisions.

BOOK	ME
12 pounds ground beef, raw	12 pounds ground beef, raw
4 cups oatmeal, uncooked	4 cups soy grits, raw
2½ cups bread, soft chopped	2 cups whole wheat bread-crumbs, soaked in milk to soften and squeezed out
5 eggs slightly beaten	5 eggs slightly beaten
5 cups tomatoes	5 cups tomatoes
5 cups cream sauce, heavy (¾ cup fat, 1 cup flour, 5 cups milk)	5 cups cream sauce, heavy (¾ cup oil, ½ cup whole wheat flour, 5 cups milk, 2 cups milk powder or 5 cups evaporated milk)
5 tablespoons salt	5 tablespoons salt
¾ teaspoons pepper	¾ teaspoon pepper
	½ cup nutritional yeast
2½ cups celery, diced	2½ cups celery
½ cup green pepper, diced	½ cup green pepper, diced
	1 cup wheat germ

Now these revisions, as you can see, are only nutritional ones. You can also see, probably, that either recipe would be *terrible* —the bland and typical institutional glop. So if I were doing it, I would triple the amount of pepper, add 2 or 3 cups chopped raw onions, several tablespoons chili powder, 2 or 3 cloves raw pressed garlic. The thing is, you can't season food as highly as you usually do, because then you would be using ⅔ cups cayenne, etc, etc, and seasonings are expensive. So, what you do is mix up the recipe ahead of time and let stand, refrigerated most likely, for a few hours, to let the seasonings you *have* added pass into the food. You know how this works—haven't you ever had a dish which you noticed tasted better reheated, or on the second or third day after cooking? So, with nutritional revisions, substitute about ¾ or a bit more of the amount of white flour called for with whole wheat. Use soy grits instead of oatmeal or other binders, and use it, along with wheat germ, for a topping on casseroles instead of bread crumbs. Enrich everything you can with nutritional yeast and noninstant powdered milk and wheat germ. Use raw sugar, a little less than they advise, when sugar is called for, and use oil instead of fat. Of *course* use things like brown rice instead of white and omit baking soda from all recipes, using baking powder or nothing at all (in most cookies, leavening really isn't required). In general, try and follow the basic nutritional rules I have laid on you all through this; with seasoning revisions, you're on your own. Remember that as far as I can tell, all recipes in quantity cooking need heavier spicing and that the seasonings will pass into foods if just mixed in and allowed to stand refrigerated.

Now, back to quantity cooking in general. There are only two more things I have to say about it. First, it can't be nearly as artistic or creative or personal an enterprise as regular cooking. A pinch of this or that won't do a thing; a garnish will have to be really massive before it commands notice in the least. Please don't forget this or you'll be very disappointed when you cook for a crowd. Second, large groups of people, to my experience, *always* eat less than you think they will. This is another strange and elusive fact of quantity cooking and one I am at loss to explain. Perhaps people eat less food cooked in quantity than in small batches because it doesn't taste as good. I really don't know. But at any rate, you can always count on having leftovers, so you'd better have some idea of what to do with them. Either you have freezer space, or you've fixed something plain so you can cream it and curry it and fricassee it for the next week.

Well, this is what we eight people bought for our first month's staples. (I didn't remember, we had a list.) It might be helpful to you.

25 pounds brown rice	5 pounds lentils
25 pounds whole wheat flour	5 pounds soybeans
10 pounds kasha	5 pounds raisins
10 pounds honey	5 pounds pinto beans
10 pounds raw sugar	2 pounds dried apricots
10 pounds brown sugar	2 pounds dried prunes
10 pounds noninstant	2 pounds soy flour
powdered milk	1 pound nutritional yeast
5 pounds couscous	1 gallon corn oil
5 pounds rye grain	1 quart olive oil
5 pounds rye flour	

Everything on this list has been eaten many times and replenished many times except a few grains, which are dwindling slowly. Nothing on it turned out to be impractical, but that's for us. It might well be impractical for you.

Chopped beef and chicken are the cheapest animal protein products. Keep them frozen because most meats spoil very quickly even when refrigerated. Thaw the night before.

You will probably need to get staples every month or two and meat, vegetable and dairy products weekly. The dairy products we generally get are:

3-6 dozen eggs	Cottage cheese
1 pound salted butter	Cream cheese
1 pound sweet butter	Sour cream
Cheese—a lot—muenster,	Yogurt
cheddar and another one,	
usually, each week	

The meat and vegetables vary from week to week. But generally we are people with contented stomachs.

shopping

where to shop

We have found places to shop that suit our needs remarkably well, and hence, if you follow this cookbook, yours. These are only for the New York area, but if you look around you can find others, I'm sure, in other places. Some of the places we go to, the specialty shops in particular, do a brisk mail order business, I'm sure. You might write and ask them for a price list.

Years and years ago Mayor La Guardia took all the pushcarts and vendors off the streets of New York and ensconced them in huge brick buildings scattered around the city. One of these is the *Essex Market,* on Essex and Delancey Streets. It is four blocks long, and awesome, especially at first. It is crammed with vegetable stands, meat stands, fruit stands, dairy counters, everything and anything. There are stands that specialize only in potatoes—others only in Chinese or Puerto Rican food. Fan*tas*tic! Chinese and Jewish and Spanish mingle, pinching fruit and getting yelled at alike by the crabby vendors. You can get *very* fresh vegetables—you can shake the water off them. While the prices are not drastically cheaper than anywhere else (*see* Hunts Point), the atmosphere is groovy. You can make friends with the vendors and then shopping is not a drag but something to look forward to.

Bernie is the dairy man. He looks like someone's uncle. He is amazing and efficient in his white apron, cutting off exactly a pound of cheese. I get a good feeling watching everything pile up—the cheeses, eggs, fresh butter cut from a *huge* tub, the yogurt and ricotta. He cuts the cheese we order and then gives us tiny delicious slivers of it to eat on our way.

Louie and Goldie are also our friends. Not quite accidentally (their string beans seemed particularly nice) we chose their vegetable stand out of the thousands there, the first time we went. We were pretty disorganized that first time and found we had forgotten something so we went back to their stand. Goldie recognized us. "Hey Louie!" she yelled. "Hey, they want a cawleeflower, give 'em a cawleeflower, they came back!" From then on we've been friends. They tell us what's good that day and give us free tastes. Crisp string beans, handfuls of sour cooking cherries, sweet new raw peas. Once Goldie gave us each a slice of cantaloupe, honey sweet. Another time she halved a beautiful tomato for us, salted it, and gave it to us to eat like an apple. Delicious! Prices of most things are something nine—29, 39, 49—they round it down for us 25, 35, 45. And when they add the whole thing up, they usually take off another fifteen cents or a dollar. Another thing they do is turn us on to rare vegetables, kohlrabi, for instance. It is a strange-looking cabbage-colored vegetable, shaped like a top. "Try it," they said, "lots of vitamins." "Okay," we said, "But how do we cook it?" "Boil it. Eat it with lots of salt and butter. Delicious." So we took it home, and it was! I didn't think it tasted like a potato, though, but Karen, Ronnie's sister, did. Crispin and Michael thought it tasted like broccoli. I thought it tasted like cabbage.

Louie and Goldie are now on vacation. They were going to Rome, to Israel, all over Europe they told me. I told them, joking, that besides being jealous, where would I get such nice vegetables? Louie smiled. "Hey, Harry!" he yelled, at the top of his voice, "Harreeeee!!" A man looked up, way across the market. Louie beckoned him. "My brother," he said to me, "Now, look," he said to Harry. "She's a nice girl who likes nice vegetables. Tell her what's good, give her time to pick out what she wants, and take care of her while I'm away."

HUNTS POINT *see* How to Live Without Very Much Money (or maybe for free).

PETE'S SPICE AND EVERYTHING NICE is at First Avenue between 10th and 11th Streets, close to the center of the hip part of the Lower East Side. It's usually jammed with people, mostly hairy, but they do business in an efficient, fast way. They are pretty expensive, but their stuff is of good quality. They carry whole-grain flours of every kind, sold in bulk, as well as beans and nuts and dried fruits and teas and honeys and health foods and cookbooks and God knows what all. The place has a delicious smell, and while the people who work there are generally more brusque than at the Essex Market, all are pleasant and some are even nice. Most of the healthful ingredients called for here will be found there, with the exception of raw organic fruits and vegetables. One thing that they have which is cheaper than most places are spices, which they carry in bulk. If you go there, get a bag of crunchy granola, a delicious breakfast cereal, and healthful.

specialty shops

TRINACRIA at Third Avenue and 29th Street, is an incredible little store. It has been written up in at least two books about New York that I know of, *The Underground Gourmet* and the *Un-Super Market Guide.* It's *still* incredible.

It's basically an Italian specialty store. Its prices are very expensive and it's certainly not within the range of average spending, but if you ever have a little extra money, or are giving a party with Italian food, this is the place. You can get a particularly good selection for an antipasto—paper-thin slices of prosciutto and salami, delicious provolone, and jars full of marinated artichokes, olives, etc, etc. They have every imaginable shape of noodle in the world and every type of jam, jelly, and preserve. They are not only Italian, but have a sprinkling of Indian, Greek and Middle Eastern and Puerto Rican foods. They also have specialty cooking equipment, pretty little enamel gravy boats, mortar and pestles, etc. They have amoretti, very sweet Italian macaroons, and dried fruits and nuts and halvah, and all sorts of things! If you have an out-of-town friend (and a lot of money) this would be the ideal place to put together an outasite Care package.

If you come to do your buying around lunch time, have one of their amazing hero sandwiches, the best I've ever had. They have hot or cold, veal and pepper, sausage, meatball—everything.

CASA MONEO, at 210 West 14th Street, is right in the heart of an area with many Spanish restaurants and stores, of which it is one. Wind your way past rosaries, Spanish love comics, jewelry and records, to the back of the store which is filled with Mexican specialties. Tortillas are what we usually go for—they are a dozen for 35 cents, I believe. They also have many different kinds of very hot peppers, guava shells in syrup, Spanish candy, and corn husks for wrapping tamales in.

how to shop

The first thing about shopping, as mentioned earlier, is to make friends with the people you will be dealing with. There are many good secondary reasons, but the first is simply that it will be more pleasant for both of you. The secondary ones are things like the grocer giving you dented cans of things free, the butcher cutting out bones and chopping things for you, the vegetable man telling you what's in season and giving you wilted vegetables free. Now, none of those are to be sneezed at—but the other is really more important.

Another thing that will happen if you make friends is you will be able to get credit if necessary. It may even be offered to you. It's better not to take it—it leads to all sorts of hassles if you're not careful.

Okay, now. Say the local merchants are all on your side. What else do you need to know? Well . . . Find out what's in season. It will taste better, and cost less. Have a list made up before you go. And follow it! Allow yourself perhaps one item off the list. The exception to this rule is if you see a truly extraordinary bargain. In general, especially if you're on the poor side, you should keep half an eye out for them. I don't mean you should call every supermarket in the city—just glance at the newspapers, or listen to one of those all-news radio stations which have periodic reports. Buy the size you need. It's as stupid to buy something too big as something too little though we generally hear it the other way. Take into account such mundane things as refrigerator space. Keep in mind that *generally, the more processed the item is, the more expensive, and less healthy* it will be. You have to decide if it's worth it. Also —beware of packaging. The capitalists are good at fooling people. My mother got this pastrami that cost 59 cents for a package which seemed big. After opening it and unwrapping it through two more layers of plastic she found 3 scrawny slices of pastrami.

what you can do
with food
besides eat it

This book is nearly finished, and I'd like to leave you with a bit of philosophy, very practical. That is, waste nothing, or almost nothing.

BONE BEADS Some of the American Indians did this. They, of course, wasted nothing.

Save all the leg bones from chicken and turkey. Boil them in water for a long time, changing the water fairly often. When most of the meat and markings have been boiled away and the bones are fairly white cool them and take them out. Saw off the knobs on the ends and slice the bones into lengths from a half to two inches. Continue boiling them. Remove from heat and take out the bones. Hold each to your lips and suck in (or blow out) any of the jelly-like marrow that may be inside. Let them cool again. Now, attach string or a thin braid of yarn to the back of a chair. Rub the string with soapy water. Let the beads soak for a while in soapy water. Then, one by one, take them out, thread the string through them and rub up and down very hard for a few minutes. The purpose of this is to get any stuff clinging to the insides of the bone out. After all the beads have been thus treated, sand each of them on the edges. Let them dry out and polish them highly. Then string them. Crispin is making me a necklace like this for my birthday.

BEAN BEADS To do this, you need an electric drill and some dried beans. I haven't experimented much but fava beans work well and soy beans don't. I think that any flat kind would work. Anyhow, drill a hole in each in about the same place, and there you are. Then string them, alternating with some other kind of bead. They're really pretty, most organic looking. Squash and pumpkin seeds also make nice beads.

HONEY-EGG FACIAL This is really great. Mix together 1 egg and about a teaspoon of honey. Spread on your face and let dry, about 5-10 minutes. Wash it off with warm, then cold water. Your face just feels fantastic. One egg is good for about 3 facials (unless you have a very big face!) and it keeps well in the refrigerator. It also doesn't feel as slimy as you might think. If it drips into your mouth, taste and swallow it. It's really good and good for you. It's not every cosmetic you can say that about. VARIATION: add lemon juice.

POTATO PRINTS Almost everyone knew about these, at one time, but most people have forgotten. First, spread a piece of paper out on a table. It should be plain colored, not printed. If it curls, weight the corners down with something. Now mix the paints, nice bright temperas mixed with water, each in a separate paper cup to make a design on the cut side. Cut-side down, dip the potato in the paint and print on the paper, in any way you like. Do it a few times in different colors and then sprinkle with another color—however you want. This makes beautiful wrapping paper—you can do a whole huge sheet in fifteen minutes.

COFFEE GRINDS, if saved and dried out, make excellent stuffing for pincushions as they are firm and keep needles and pins from rusting. They are somewhat difficult to work with though. They can be used to make interesting textural designs —use Elmer's glue to hold them.

At our house, if you spend time cooking a meal you don't

go unnoticed. People are aware and they appreciate it. For this reason, and also because you only have to cook one night a week and not clean up that night, cooking is no drag at all. No matter who cooks, meals are something special.

They're also different. One night Puerto Rican Food, the next Chinese or Indian or vegetarian or Mexican, food from Texas or New York, from all the different places that we come from. And what I'm trying to say here is, the way it is with food, it is with everything.

bibliography

additional new-life, new-world reading

The Poisons in Your Food—William Longgood. The source book on food adulteration. Absolutely terrifying, and well-documented too.

The Adelle Davis books—*Let's Eat Right to Keep Fit* (New American Library, 1970), *Let's Get Well* (Harcourt Brace Jovanovich, Inc., 1965), *Let's Cook It Right* (Harcourt Brace Jovanovich, Inc., 1962), *Let's Have Healthy Children* (Harcourt Brace Jovanovich, Inc., 1959). Although these books are somewhat repetitive and overlapping, they are the only honest and somewhat sanely written books on nutrition for the layman that I know of. In order of title they cover: general and basic nutrition, cure and prevention of various illnesses through good nutrition (what vitamin to take for what), methods of preserving nutrients (and ordinary type recipes revised to be healthful), and care and nutrition and diet and supplementation as well as advice on childcare through the preschool years.

The Natural Foods Cookbook, by Beatrice Trum Hunter

(Simon and Schuster, 1969). This cookbook grows on you. The more I use it the more impressed with it I become. Mrs. Hunter's recipes are really original and good. She uses the blender as a particularly creative tool, and has a lot of recipes for organ meats. *Warning:* don't use quite as much nutritional yeast as she says, except in breads. A lot of her stuff is too yeasty.

ALTERNATIVES:
OTHER CULTURES, COMMUNITY, ANARCHISM, LIBERATION
(how can you separate these?)

Mutual Aid—Petr Kropotkin. "Up against the history of leaders, wars, slavery, kings, wealth and poverty, courts, bureaucracies, alienating institutions, the arrogant looking down and the insipid looking up that is inherent in a society divided into classes, there is another history—a history of ordinary people building their own social organizations, constructing their own social customs and common law in order to maintain control over their every day lives, creating new social organizations to regain control whenever repressive or natural forces destroyed old ones. This book is the story of that history." Reviewed by Lynn Astons in *Roots.*

Ishi in Two Worlds—Hoebel Ishi was the last wild Indian in North America.

Anarchos—Irregular publication on anarchism as it relates to ecology, technology, you and me. Often wordy, but good. Anarchos, P. O. Box 466, Peter Stuyvesant Station, N.Y., N.Y. 10019

Whole Earth Catalog—no explanation necessary.

Roots, also irregularly published, is a journal of ecology with a radical outlook and beautiful graphics. $5.00 for ten issues, from Ecology Action East, Box 344, Cooper Station, N.Y. 10003. Write for a *free* issue if you really don't have any money.

An excellent and extensive packet on *Women's Liberation* is available from the New England Free Press, 791 Tremont Street, Boston, Mass. 02118. It costs $2.75 plus 15% for postage and handling—total cost $3.16. It includes the politics of housework—very relevant to communal cooking!

Cheyenne Autumn, by Mari Sandoz (Avon, 1969), is the story of the Cheyennes' flight from their "reservation" to their home, the story of the strength individuals draw from community, and the beauty of community, the story of the barrenness and stupidity and alienation of our "civilization"; our lack of a culture of our own and our annihilation of other cultures.

Sisterhood Is Powerful: An Anthology of Writings from the Women's Liberation Movement, collected by Robin Morgan (Random House, Paper, 1970). Very extensive and must reading.

And, though some of his stuff makes me sad because of its sexist attitude, read any of the books by Richard Brautigan.

further

This book has been written over a span of almost eight months. Things have changed a lot here during that time.

Although the original core of Big Diane, Little Diane, Mike, Ronnie, Crispin and myself has remained, many other people have passed through our doors, to live and to visit and to party, and all have exerted their effects over the house. There was Mickey, who moved in with us, but had to leave soon after, due to a trial in California about his draft status. And Dave, who came in soon after, who was quiet and sensitive and said "far-out" a lot, who danced in a big free way that all the kids used to imitate, opening their eyes wide, waving their arms and legs: "Dave dance like this, right?" always to "Crossroads" by Cream, or to Spirit, who left for Mexico when the city got to him. And Brad and Pablo, who lived here briefly, and Freddy and Boo and Vicky and Susan and Bernard and Levy (these last three a couple and their baby), who all lived here more permanently, and who in fact, lived here at this writing. We have many more people here now than we did initially. Vicky is in one living room, Big Diane in the other (she gave up her room to Bernard and Susan and Levy). But Crispin and I are leaving soon, and that will balance things out a little. Boo will take our room, Vicky will take his.

Leaving.

Leaving Brooklyn and the shady brownstone. Leaving Big Black (as opposed to Little White) Freddy, with his incredible sexism and his incredible charm, who stayed with us the night we were robbed, who complains that now, because of my preaching he *has* to have breakfast before he goes to work. Leaving the neighborhood kids, Vanessa next door with her front teeth out and her funny expressions and her beautiful silly way of laughing, and the way she said to me, her face all scrunched up with delight after we had been rolling soft cookie dough into balls, "Oooo, iz *squishy* like *mud*," and her brother James, who one day wanted to go for a ride in the jeep and so forged a note to us with a reason to go and then read it out loud in his slow, deliberate way: "Dear Crescent and Crisp, you have to go to the store in the jeep to pick up oranges and lemons, Ronnie." Innocent look. "Well, dig that." And Dennis and Annette who went with us to hear and see the Musica Electronica Viva at the Brooklyn Academy of Music and didn't have a very good time, Dennis who wants to be a vetcrinarian, who had a housebroken pet pigeon named Igor, a succession of cats, a dog with puppies and a hamster named Hippie, and his sister Annette, who made a fantastic puppet in school and who learned how to crochet faster than anyone I have ever taught, and Alida their sister, who is one of us (as are we all), who is incredibly beautiful and slim and delicate featured and (who will kill me for saying it) who danced more fluidly and easily that nearly anyone I know, and her boyfriend Nelson who is also one of us and is tall and frizzy headed and soft voiced, leaving.

Leaving the blond, busy Millers and Brooklyn Tech across the street and the pollution and the noise and the hassles with the bureaucracy and sneaking in the subway and alternate-side-of-the-street parking regulations and leaving Junior, wanting very much to swoop down and take him and Alida and Nelson and Freddy and Dennis and Annette and James and Nessa out of this ugly city to live with us in a utopia that does not yet exist: dreams of *Aftertherevolution* and Junior, with whom I spent hours rapping politics: Panthers, Lords, Women's Liberation (hardest for him to grasp—the discussion started when he said "Afeni Shakur—she's the head of the lady Panthers?"), who taught me something about my own arrogance and racism by being so far ahead of every assumption I made to myself about "neighborhood kids," until I stopped making assumptions, teaching me outright certain things, teaching me, too, by making me teach, explain and clarify things to him, who read the vows at our wedding ceremony because he is one of the most honest people we know, who baked bread with us and learned about organic food with us and danced with us if everybody was so he wasn't feeling dumb. Junior. Leaving. Really leaving.

But where to? To the country, to new worlds. With the money from this book, Crispin and I bought a farm. It's in the Ozarks and it's a beautiful farm, with a hundred and thirty-one acres, with frontage on a sparkling, dancing, pure, tree-over-hung creek, with three or four little springs and a tidy white farmhouse and rolling sensuous little hills and dips and bends and fields and woods and edible wild plants and mushrooms and snakes and rabbits and lizards and crawdads and frogs and squirrels and raccoons and butterflies and birds; a farm. Open to people who want to build a new way of life, set up an example of how things will maybe be after the revolution, people who will not be forgetting the work their brothers and sisters are doing in the city, who will be working in different, perhaps more subversive and/or subtle ways; fighting defined sex roles and male chauvinism in themselves and others; getting into the rural communities and turning on (and no doubt being turned on by) the kids, gathering skills for when things start to fall apart (and they will), building a sane, healthy place to live and have children in, beginning to think in terms of generations instead of months and I am incredibly excited about *doing it;* growing our own food, weaving our own clothes, building and creating new artistic technologies—technologies that we are not cut off from and out of touch with, technologies each of us understands and views as a part of or an extension of him or herself, technologies that do not pollute but live in sensitive balance with the environment, technologies that free us, rather than enslave us. And we will be so close to our environment and know it so well that it too will be an extension of us, as each person shall be of every other person. Come and see us; we'll be there, baring our bodies and growing strong and lean and brown and muscled side by side in the sun, fighting, changing, learning, loving. Come and see us, there's room for you, for Junior, Nelson, Alida, Nessa, James, Annette, the Brooklyn commune, Brooklyn, New York City. Come and see us, you can't miss us, if you look you'll find us, for we are everywhere and we are everyone. We are you.

index